THE POLITICS OF EDUCATION

THE POLITICS
OF EDUCATION

*Conflict and Consensus
on Capitol Hill*

BY JOHN BRADEMAS

With Lynne P. Brown

UNIVERSITY OF OKLAHOMA PRESS : NORMAN AND LONDON

BY JOHN BRADEMAS

Anarcosindicalismo y revolución en España, 1930–1937
(Barcelona, 1974)

Washington D.C. to Washington Square (New York, 1986)

The Politics of Education: Conflict and Consensus on Capitol Hill
(Norman, 1987)

Library of Congress Cataloging-in-Publication Data

Brademas, John, 1927–
    The politics of education

    (The Julian J. Rothbaum distinguished lecture series; v. 1)
    Includes bibliographical references and index.
        1. Education and state—United States.   2. Educational law and
    legislation—United States.   3. Federal aid to education—United
    States.   4. Democracy.   5. Politics and education—United States.
    I. Brown, Lynne P.   II. Title.   III. Series.
    LC111.B65   1987   379.73   86–40526
    ISBN 0–8061–2058–4 (alk. paper)

The paper in this book meets the guidelines for permanence
and durability of the Committee on Production Guidelines
for Book Longevity of the Council on Library Resources, Inc.

For my mother

CONTENTS

FOREWORD

AMONG THE MANY GOOD THINGS that have happened to me in my life, there is none in which I take more pride than the establishment of the Carl Albert Congressional Research and Studies Center at the University of Oklahoma, and none in which I take more satisfaction than the Center's presentation of the Julian J. Rothbaum Distinguished Lecture Series. The series is a perpetually endowed program of the University of Oklahoma, created in honor of Julian J. Rothbaum by his wife, Irene, and son, Joel.

Julian J. Rothbaum, my close friend since our childhood days in southeastern Oklahoma, has long been a leader in Oklahoma civic affairs. He has served as a Regent of the University of Oklahoma for two terms and as a State Regent for

Higher Education. In 1974 he was awarded the University's highest honor, the Distinguished Service Citation, and in 1986 he was inducted into the Oklahoma Hall of Fame.

The Rothbaum Lecture Series is devoted to the themes of representative government, democracy and education, and citizen participation in public affairs, values to which Julian J. Rothbaum has been committed throughout his life. His life-long dedication to the University of Oklahoma, the state, and his country is a tribute to the ideals to which the Rothbaum Lecture Series is dedicated. The books comprising the series make an enduring contribution to an understanding of American democracy.

CARL B. ALBERT

Forty-sixth Speaker
of the
United States House of Representatives

PREFACE

The genius of the collective will of the American people—from all walks of life, all races and national origins, and all religions—applied through the principles of representative democracy with proper inspiration from their leaders, can meet the challenges, large though they loom.

We, therefore, turn to our labors with confidence and determination. We cannot falter; we will not fail.

—CARL ALBERT, QUOTED IN THE *Congressional Record*, JANUARY 21, 1971

I HAD BEEN A MEMBER OF CONGRESS a dozen years when, on January 21, 1971, Carl Albert of Oklahoma spoke these words as he rose to accept the votes of his colleagues to become the forty-sixth Speaker of the United States House of Representatives, a position he appropriately described as "the chosen leader of the people's branch of Government."

When I was invited, yet another dozen years later, to the University of Oklahoma and the Carl Albert Congressional Research and Studies Center to deliver the first Julian J. Rothbaum Lectures in Representative Government, I invoked this statement of Speaker Albert's because I felt it both summarized the spirit that brought together that week political leaders and university officials, students and teachers and served as fitting prologue to my talks on politics, education, and the national interest.

Although they have been modified to take subsquent developments into account, my lectures delivered in Norman, Oklahoma, in the fall of 1983 form the basis of this book. My
topic, simply put, is the politics of federal support for education. More specifically, I explore the making of education policy during my years in the House of Representatives and then
suggest both current themes of and future directions for education policy that may (or may not) flow from the legislative
history of which I was a part.

I must caution the reader that I write from a highly personal
perspective, that of a practicing politician who was for twenty-
two years a member of the committee of the House with principal responsibility for education legislation and who now, as
leader of the largest private university in the nation, is concerned with the education of over 46,000 students. I am not,
nor do I choose to be, or be seen to be, a detached observer.

Nor do I make an attempt in these pages to be exhaustive in
my analysis. Rather I rely on selective examples, drawn from
my experience as lawmaker and university president, to convey to the reader a sense of the processes and personalities
that help shape public policy toward education. This is not a
primer for understanding how our laws are made; it is one
person's account of how certain laws were made at certain
times.

In the first chapter I look through the prism of my own life
to show connections between education and politics and indi-
cate how for Congress and the nation education emerged as a
focus of federal action. In the next three chapters I sift through
two decades of experience in Congress to illustrate how specific pieces of education legislation were developed and, more
generally, to identify the factors and forces that animate the
legislative process in the American political system. Sir Nich-
olas Henderson, a former British ambassador to the United
States, once observed of his American cousins: "You don't
have a system of government. You have a maze." Chapters 2 to
4 are efforts to impose some structure and pattern on the

labyrinthine ways of Congress, especially of the House of Representatives.

Over the past few years there has been a dramatic resurgence of interest in education in this country. The American people have come increasingly to recognize that what happens in our schools, colleges, and universities—or does not happen—directly affects the strength of our economy, the security of our borders, and the quality of our national life. In a time of intensifying concern, what new steps ought we to be taking to improve our educational system? What are the responsibilities of the various sectors of society in bringing about change? Where will we get the money to pay for education? These are vital questions for the 1980s and beyond.

They are questions that cannot be considered apart from the political scene. For education involves both values and resources, and in a democratic society the joining of values and resources leads to politics.

Since I delivered the Rothbaum Lectures, the nation has overwhelmingly reelected Ronald Reagan president of the United States. The implications of that choice for federal policy toward education are profound. For the two candidates for the highest office in the land in 1984 pressed wholly different views on the role of government in support of teaching and learning.

It is essential to keep in mind, however, that in November, 1984, the voters chose not only a president and a vice-president but also one-third of the Senate and the entire House of Representatives. The process, on the congressional level, was repeated in 1986. The shape of public policy, including education policy, revolves around not only what a president wants but also what he can get from a Senate and a House that may be controlled by parties different from his own.

Chapters 5 and 6 bring into sharper focus the themes and concerns that have emerged from the recent debate on education and then examine prominent features of the political and economic landscape that will determine whether and, if so, how those themes are translated into concrete proposals for action.

Chapters 7 and 8 venture onto philosophical ground with some thoughts on the relationship between education and democracy. Since the founding of the Republic, Americans have looked to our institutions of learning to prepare students to live as citizens of a free, self-governing country. At a time when it is not difficult to find signs of our failure as a nation to understand the languages and cultures of other peoples of the world and even of how our own system of government works, I think it imperative to examine the question of education for citizenship.

I should here note that portions of chapters 5 and 7 have appeared in different form in speechs I have delivered on similar topics.

I must here express my gratitude to those who inspired and organized the Rothbaum Lectures. First, my thanks go to the distinguished Oklahoman in whose name they were given. A long-time friend and benefactor of the University of Oklahoma, Julian Rothbaum has dedicated a lifetime to encouraging thoughtful citizen participation in public affairs; to be asked to inaugurate a program bearing his name was an honor. Together with Mr. Rothbaum, Mrs. Rothbaum and her son, Joel Jankowsky, a valued friend from the days we both served on Capitol Hill, have created in the Rothbaum Lectures a significant forum for the discussion of representative institutions and democratic values. I also warmly thank my hosts during my visit at the university, then President William S. Banowsky and especially Ronald Peters, Director of the Carl Albert Center.

I am particularly grateful to Lynne P. Brown, a member of my staff in Washington when I was House Majority Whip and who continues to work with me at New York University. Dr. Brown, a political scientist who has studied majority leadership in the U.S. House of Representatives, has been of great, indeed, invaluable, assistance to me in producing this volume. I wish also to thank Mark Adams Taylor for his skillful research and Susan Feldman for keeping the project on track.

To my former colleagues in Congress, from whom I learned much about the themes of this book—politics, democracy, and education—I am deeply appreciative.

Finally, I offer a special tribute to the distinguished American under whose leadership I spent most of my years of service as a member of Congress—a knowledgeable mentor and a legislator with a gift for harmonizing differences and building coalitions for constructive action—the Honorable Carl Albert.

New York City   JOHN BRADEMAS
January, 1987

PART ONE

THE EVOLUTION OF FEDERAL AID
TO EDUCATION, 1959–1980

CHAPTER 1

THE FEDERAL ROLE IN EDUCATION:
A PERSONAL PERSPECTIVE

OVER A GENERATION AGO one of my professors at Harvard began his lectures by warning the students: "First, I'd better tell you what I believe. I believe in sweet reason, high morality, and plenty of horsepower!" In like fashion I should explain my origins so that the reader will understand, if not always share, my views.

As the son of a Greek immigrant and a Hoosier schoolteacher of Scots–English–Irish–Pennsylvania Dutch ancestry, I grew up with a foot in each of two different cultures. My father, like many other newly arrived Greeks of his era, went into the restaurant business. My mother, daughter of an Indiana high school superintendent and college professor, chose the classroom and for nearly half a century was a teacher in the public schools of Indiana and Michigan.

During my childhood in the Midwest my brothers and sister and I spent the summer months in my grandparents' home in Swayzee, a small Indiana town, where we were exposed both to my grandfather's keen interest in history and politics and to his library, which had nearly ten times more volumes, seven thousand, than Swayzee had residents. I practically lived in that library, and those books enabled me to travel, in my mind, far beyond the borders of north-central Indiana. I was therefore reared in a family for whom education was paramount, and so intense was my father's commitment that he used to say, "John, I'll never leave much money to my children but I will leave you all a first-class education." That education began for me in local public schools—James Madison Elementary and Central High, in South Bend.

Beyond the influence of family was that of the Methodist church. Although my father was Greek Orthodox and my mother belonged to the Disciples of Christ, the Brademas children, in ecumenical spirit, joined the Methodist church. American Methodism has long been characterized by a strong sense of social concern, and my membership in the Methodist church greatly affected my attitudes, especially on such issues as civil rights, from my days in school through university and into Congress.

The views I developed in school were reinforced in my freshman year, as a naval officer candidate, at the University of Mississippi. There in the spring of 1946 I heard the late Senator Theodore G. Bilbo open his final campaign in the Faulknerian town of Pontotoc. Bilbo's words were so virulently racist—he lashed out at "Clare Booth Luce and those other Communists [sic] up North who want to mongrelize the white race"—that I wondered if the Senator was unaware that the nation had been at war with the Japanese and Germans and was not engaged in a replay of the War Between the States.

That experience quickened my fascination with politics, and at Harvard, where I studied after Ole Miss, I majored in government. I spent one summer as an intern at the United Nations, then at Lake Success, and another in the mountains of Mexico in a kind of forerunner of the Peace Corps, as one of a group of American college students who helped the local Indians improve their crop yields, vaccinated them against disease, and with them built a children's playground. In Mexico I practiced my Spanish and found inspiration for what was to be my Harvard honors thesis on a right-wing Mexican peasant movement.

Harvard was for me four years (1946–50) in a magnificent treasure house of ideas and people. Not only did I study under great teachers—men like Samuel Beer, Raphael Demos, William Yandell Elliott, Carl Friedrich, Alvin Hansen, Louis Hartz, and Perry Miller—but I learned as well from the bright, intense students of the postwar generation.

A Rhodes scholarship at Oxford, an opportunity I shared— years later—with Carl Albert, opened another cornucopia of people and ideas as well as new places to visit—England, Scotland, France, my father's Greece. Yet I was drawn to Spain and stimulated by that seminal study of the social and economic background of the Spanish Civil War, *The Spanish Labyrinth* of Gerald Brenan, I decided to write a doctoral dissertation on the anarchist movement in Catalonia from 1923 through mid-1937, the first year of the Civil War.

My research was carried out in large part through interviews I conducted in London and in Paris and other cities in France with Spanish anarchists in exile from their home country and eager to talk to a young scholar about their ideology and experiences. Spain was the only country in the world that saw the rise of a large working-class movement reared not on the ideas of Karl Marx but on those of Mikhail Bakunin and other anarchist thinkers.

My interest in the Hispanic world continues to this day at New York University, which has one of the strongest programs of Spanish studies of any American university. Indeed, in December, 1983, I was privileged to bestow an honorary degree on His Majesty King Juan Carlos I of Spain and to announce the creation of a chair in Spanish culture and civilization in the name of this young leader of the new Spanish democracy.[1]

[1]Other symbols of the growing commitment of New York University to the study of Hispanic culture and civilization include the conferral of honorary degrees, in 1984, on the distinguished Mexican poet and essayist Octavio Paz and, in 1985, on Raúl Alfonsín, president of Argentina, who is courageously leading his country back into the family of free and democratic nations.

While I was in England completing my dissertation and wondering what I would do on my return to the United States, I considered three options: pursuing a career in the Foreign Service or the United Nations, becoming a Hispanic scholar, or running for Congress. This was a time, the summer of 1953, of turubulent politics in the United States. The newspapers were filled with accounts of the assaults of Senator Joseph McCarthy, the Wisconsin Republican, on, among other groups, the United States Foreign Service, and I decided that the life of a professional diplomat, constrained to suffer such senatorial abuse in silence, was not for me. I wanted to be where I could talk back.

I postponed a decision on what to do by starting law school, thinking that in a few years' time I would run for Congress. But I determined to take the political plunge somewhat earlier and, in 1954, at the age of twenty-six, sought a seat in the U.S. House of Representatives from my home district, Indiana's third, centering around South Bend. With the support and counsel of the late Paul M. Butler, of South Bend, then Democratic national committeeman from Indiana and later chairman of the Democratic National Committee, I won the nomination in a field of several candidates.

In the general election I lost to the Republican incumbent by five-tenths of a percentage point. Naturally, I decided to run again in 1956. During 1955–56, however, I worked in Chicago in the second presidential campaign of Adlai E. Stevenson as his executive assistant in charge of research on issues. Both Stevenson and Brademas lost their races in the Eisenhower landslide of 1956.

As preached—and practiced—by Adlai Stevenson, politics was a noble pursuit, calling on all the resources of mind and character an individual could muster. Stevenson's was an unshakable faith in the proposition that ideas can make a difference in public life, and his example had a profound influence on me as a young man just undertaking such a career.

Still convinced that I could go to Congress, I ran a third time and, after a year and a half of teaching political science at Saint Mary's College, Notre Dame, I was elected in 1958. The following January, I was sworn in as a freshman member of the Eighty-sixth Congress.

As this brief sketch makes clear, the two strands of education and politics were firmly woven into the experiences of my youth and young adulthood. By the time I entered Congress, at the age of thirty-one, I already had deeply felt views about education and its place on the national agenda. First, I was convinced that education was indispensable to happiness as defined by the Greeks: "the exercise of vital powers along lines of excellence in a life affording them scope."

Second, education not only had expanded my own capacities but was demonstrably a ladder to social and economic advance. That the son of an Indiana schoolteacher and a Greek immigrant should have been able to study at the two finest universities in the world impressed deeply upon me the significance of an opportunity for education.

Beyond an appreciation of the power of education to shape an individual's skills and values and to enhance one's mobility in society, I had by the time I went into politics another conviction: that education was at the foundation of our hopes for building a nation strong both in economic and material terms and in the quality of our intellectual and cultural life.

The year of my third and successful bid for Congress, 1958, was also a momentous one in both education and politics in this country. In that year, under the leadership of President Eisenhower, Congress approved legislation that signaled a new federal role in education—the National Defense Education Act (NDEA).

The environment for this pioneering measure had already been shaped by a century and a half of involvement by the national government in education. The history of federal support for education shows a gradual adaptation to the changing needs and aspirations of a growing nation. The benchmarks of that evolution are well known:

1. As early as 1787, Congress specified that a portion of federal land ceded to the states in the Northwest Territories be reserved to support local public schools.
2. Nearly a century later the Morrill Act distributed federal land to the states "to establish colleges for the benefit of agriculture and mechanic arts."
3. The GI Bill of World War II, the most sweeping program of federal aid to education ever enacted, afforded millions of returning veterans—of whom I was one—the means to go to college.

Each era has produced its own stimulus and rationale for the use of federal tax dollars to assist education. In the eighteenth century one motive was expressed in these words of the Northwest Ordinance of 1787: ". . . religion, morality, and knowledge being necessary to good government and the happiness of mankind, schools and the means of education shall forever be encouraged." The movement toward land-grant colleges in the 1860s took place in the context of America's entrance into the technological age and the need to prepare students in the sciences, the mechanical arts, and agricultural and other skills essential to that time. The GI Bill arose from a sense of national obligation to those who had defended the country but also had the effect of averting severe economic dislocations that might have accompanied the sudden entrance into the labor force of hundreds of thousands of returning soldiers.

In 1958 the justification for an expanded federal role in education was found in a small, 184-pound sphere orbiting the earth once every ninety minutes. For the Soviets' launching of the world's first man-made satellite, *Sputnik I,* on October 4, 1957, not only sparked the beginning of a race to space but set in motion political forces that were to alter profoundly the relationship of the federal government to the nation's schools, colleges, and universities.

With the passage of the National Defense Education Act a new federal purpose in education was articulated:

> The Congress hereby finds and declares that the security of the nation requires the fullest development of the mental resources and technical skills of its young men and women. . . . The national interest requires . . . that the federal government give assistance to education for programs which are important to our national defense. [PL 85-864, sec. 401]

The NDEA provided federal funds to improve the teaching of mathematics, science, and foreign languages in both schools and universities, as well as money for college student loans and graduate fellowships and awards for university-based research. James L. Sundquist, one of the most perceptive analysts of federal education policy, concludes that the significance of the NDEA came not from its specific provisions but because "it asserted more forcefully than at any time in nearly a century, a national interest in the quality of education that the states, communities, and private institutions provide."[2]

I entered Congress the year following enactment of the NDEA. The year 1958 had been a very good one for the Democratic party. After 1954, when, following two years of Republican rule, the Democrats won back control of both the House and the Senate, Democratic majorities grew steadily. The 1958 elections brought forty-nine more Democrats to the House and fifteen more to the Senate (the party ratios for the Eighty-sixth Congress were, in the House, 283 Democrats and 153 Republicans, and, in the Senate, 64 Democrats and 34 Republicans).

As a newly elected congressman, I realized that my most important decision was my committee assignment. It is chiefly

[2]James L. Sundquist, *Politics and Policy* (Washington, D.C.: Brookings Institution, 1968), p. 179.

through work on committees that a representative builds his or her reputation and exercises influence. At the suggestion of the late D. B. Hardeman of Texas, a senior House aide, after the November, 1958, elections I traveled to a small town in the northeast corner of Texas to call on one of the towering figures in the nation's political life, Sam Rayburn, the Speaker of the House of Representatives. Rayburn lived in a white frame house just off the side of the road in Bonham. He and his sister had invited me for lunch, and after the meal, sitting in a rocker in his living room, the Speaker addressed me with blunt friendliness: "I s'pose you want to talk about your committee?"

"Yes, sir," I replied. "Mr. Speaker, I'd like to be on the Education and Labor Committee."

"Hazardous committee, hazardous committee!" the Speaker rejoined, referring to the controversial issues—and personalities—that characterized the committee. I said I realized that but thought it an important assignment nonetheless because the issues that legislative panel would be considering would have a major impact on the people I represented in northern Indiana (in my district were the regional campuses of two state universities, Indiana University and Purdue; the University of Notre Dame; and Saint Mary's, Goshen, and Bethel colleges). Moreover, I said, I believed that in the years ahead the federal government would be giving much more attention to education.

Speaker Rayburn was not in the habit of issuing guarantees to freshman congressmen, but when committees were named, I drew my first choice, Education and Labor, and remained on the committee throughout my service in Congress.

The committee seat I came to hold—second-ranking member of the elementary and secondary subcommittee—had previously been occupied by a congressman from Massachusetts who had left the House to run successfully for the Senate and who, in two years' time would occupy still higher office—John F. Kennedy. As president, Kennedy was a vigorous advocate of federal support for education. Although his aspirations for a general school-aid bill were frustrated during his administration, his legacy includes several measures signed into law in the weeks after his assassination—for medical and dental education, college academic facilities, and vocational education.[3]

The most prodigious outpouring of education legislation came, of course, following the election of 1964, under the leadership of Lyndon Baines Johnson. I recall, when I was in Austin in 1971 for the dedication of the LBJ Library, how the former president, with a granddaughter perched on his shoulder, greeted me after the ceremonies. He said, referring to a suite in the library adjacent to the replica of the Oval Office, "Johnny, I want you to go up to the eighth floor and look at the pens I used to sign all those education bills you and I wrote." I did look; under a glass-topped table were dozens of pens.

There are some who say, in light of the fragmentary and incremental way in which presidents and Congresses inevitably make policy, that those of us—both Presidents Kennedy and Johnson and we in Congress who supported them—did not really understand what we were doing when we wrote those laws. Not so. We who worked in committee and on the floor to fashion legislative measures to support education and other activities of the mind and imagination had clear and, for us, compelling objectives. Certainly our original intent was not always translated with precision into the final legislative prod-

[3]For a useful collection of John F. Kennedy's statements and views on education during his years as a congressman, senator, and president, see William T. O'Hara, ed., *John F. Kennedy on Education* (New York: Teachers College Press, Columbia University, 1966). In the introduction to O'Hara's work, which I wrote while I was in Congress, I trace Kennedy's legislative achievements (and setbacks) on education policy. Of course, the roots of many of the federal education programs of the 1960s extend back still further, to Franklin D. Roosevelt and the New Deal. See John Brademas, "The Education Dimension of the New Deal Legacy," in Wilbur J. Cohen, ed., *The New Deal: Fifty Years Later* (Austin: Lyndon Baines Johnson Library and LBJ School of Public Affairs, University of Texas, 1984).

uct. Lawmaking in our system is too messy and porous for exact outcomes. Furthermore, a legislator who is effective *learns* in the process of legislating and, in response to new information and new ideas, often moves away from first judgments. Nonetheless, I can identify during the time of my service in Congress the commitments that informed my approach—and that of many of my colleagues as well as presidents—to the legislation we passed. Such aims may impose a pattern on the seemingly bewildering array of measures enacted in the years from 1959 to 1980.

First, we—and when I say "we," I include presidents, senators, and representatives of both parties—made a commitment to make education accessible to those otherwise likely to be excluded. Obviously, I think here of the Elementary and Secondary Education Act of 1965 (ESEA), which for the first time provided substantial federal funds to grade schools and high schools, with particular attention to the teaching of disadvantaged children. The financial fulcrum of that act is Title I (now Chapter 1), which provides federal funds to school districts with large numbers of low-income children.

In addition to ESEA, Lyndon Johnson's proudest jewel, there were as well Project Head Start, the Job Corps, the Neighborhood Youth Corps, Upward Bound, and all the other components of the War on Poverty. There were also the vocational education and manpower-training initiatives and a measure on which I labored long, the Education for All Handicapped Children Act. Each of these programs grew out of a deep concern of many of us about the education of children who were particularly vulnerable.

And to expand the opportunities for a college education, presidents of both parties—Eisenhower, Kennedy, Johnson, Nixon, Ford, and Carter—as well as Democrats and Republicans in Congress, created, from the National Defense Education Act of 1958 through a series of higher education laws, a fabric of grants, loans and work-study jobs for talented and motivated but needy young men and women.

We made a second commitment during my time in Washington: to support our institutions of culture. The milestones along this path included the National Endowments for the Arts and the Humanities as well as programs to assist libraries. I was proud to be a champion of these measures on Capitol Hill and to sponsor other programs, such as assistance for museums.

There was a third commitment: to strengthen international studies in our colleges and universities. Here I cite the International Education Act of 1966 as well as other efforts to encourage teaching and learning about the peoples and cultures of the rest of the world.

A fourth commitment was to research. Support from the national government has been crucial in enhancing our understanding of ourselves and our universe through, among other entities, the National Science Foundation, the National Institutes of Health, and the National Institute of Education. I felt a special commitment to the last initiative. When I introduced the bill to create the National Institute of Education, substantial percentages of the annual federal budgets for defense, agriculture, and health were earmarked for research and development. Yet when it came to education, which has such an enormous impact on our society, the nation was not spending the small amount needed to generate thoughtful, objective, analytical evidence concerning how people teach and learn.

These four commitments, then, guided and informed our actions as lawmakers for education. But good intentions are not enough. Where do such ideas come from, and how are they translated into the law of the land? It is to finding answers to these questions that the following chapters will be devoted.

CHAPTER 2

CONGRESS AND THE SOURCES
OF POLICY

THE MAKING OF LEGISLATIVE POLICY starts with ideas. What is their source, and how do the ideas enter the minds of congressmen and senators?

The origins of legislation are not always clear; they are often the product of many persons and many factors, from both within and without government, over many years. In his classic study *Congressional Government*, Woodrow Wilson, then professor of government at The Johns Hopkins University, observed that legislation "is an aggregate, not a simple production. It is impossible to tell how many persons, opinions, and influences have entered into its composition."[1]

It is a commonplace to observe that since the days of President Wilson the chief executive has also become chief legislator, the most important fount of bills considered by Congress. This is often but not always the case. One of my purposes in this chapter is to explain how in certain circumstances Congress, which is after all the lawmaking branch of the government, may be the principal provenance of legislative proposals.

---

[1] Woodrow Wilson, *Congressional Government: A Study in American Politics* (Boston: Houghton-Mifflin, 1885; New York: Meridian Books, 1956), p. 208.

14

THE PRESIDENT AS LEGISLATIVE LEADER: ESEA

Let me nonetheless begin with an example of an audacious initiative of the executive branch. Without question one of the most significant education measures ever enacted was proposed by President Lyndon B. Johnson with his call for what came to be the Elementary and Secondary Education Act of 1965.

For twenty years before Johnson's presidency proponents of federal aid for public schools had failed in their efforts to pass such legislation. There were three principal obstacles: segregation, religion, and Republicans.[2] Many Republicans, and some conservative Democrats, feared that federal aid would inevitably mean federal control of what was taught in the schools. Southern Democrats opposed any attempt to prohibit assistance to segregated schools. Representatives with strong Roman Catholic constituencies rejected any measure that outlawed funds for parochial schools. This combination of factors provided effective in killing general aid to schools until two developments: in 1964 Lyndon Johnson was elected president, and large Democratic majorities were returned to the House and Senate.[3]

[2] In his analysis of the impediments to passage of federal education legislation in the late 1940s and 1950s, Richard Fenno also points to the House Education and Labor Committee itself. The volatile personalities and political cleavages that characterized the committee, says Fenno, worked against the conflict resolution and consensus building needed to craft legislation in committee and form majorities for it on the floor. Far from overcoming the obstacles of Republican disapproval and segregationist and religious fears about education aid, committee members only exacerbated these divisions. See Richard Fenno, "The House of Representatives and Federal Aid to Education," in Robert L. Peabody and Nelson W. Polsby, eds., *New Perspectives on the House of Representatives,* 2d. ed. (Chicago: Rand McNally, 1969).

[3] The composition of the Education and Labor Committee also shifted in a more liberal direction. In 1959, reflecting the significant change in party alignments as a result of the 1958 elections, in which Democrats gained 49 seats in the House of Representatives, the House Democratic Caucus set the party ratio for the committee at 20 Democrats and 10 Republicans (from the previous 17-13 ratio), and six new nonsouthern Democrats from the more lib-

Within weeks after the election Johnson decided to make federal help to schools a central feature of his 1965 domestic program. The major task of shaping a proposal was assigned to Francis Keppel, former dean of the Graduate School of Education at Harvard and at the time United States commissioner of education. Keppel began negotiations with the principal groups, especially the National Catholic Welfare Conference[4] and the National Education Association, that had contended over federal aid before with such divisive consequences. Some members of Congress were also consulted, but the White House believed that, if an agreement could be worked out among the groups that had, in the past, exerted such strong crosscutting pressures on Congress the way would be cleared for legislative acceptance of whatever compromise could be developed outside Congress.

Because I had good relations with Keppel stemming from our Harvard link; with the president of the NEA, Robert Wyatt, who was head of its Indiana affiliate and a home-state political ally of mine; and with Monsignor Frederick Hochwalt of the NCWC (I represented the district in which the University of Notre Dame was situated), I arranged some private dinners at which these leaders were able to explore the issues and assess possible areas of compromise. Eugene Eidenberg and Roy D. Morey, whose book *An Act of Congress: The Legislative Process and the Making of Education Policy*[5] chronicles the history of the ESEA, found these meetings crucial to the final evolution of the 1965 act. They provided an opportunity for representatives of the key forces to express their views candidly and for the administration to determine the limits within which a bill would have to be crafted. The breakthrough in the

---

eral wing of the party were assigned to the committee. Ibid., p. 293. I was one of the new members.

[4] Now the United States Catholic Conference.

[5] New York: W. W. Norton and Co., 1969, pp. 83–84.

church-state controversy came with the acceptance of a "child-benefit" concept, which held that aid was meant not for the schools themselves but for the children in the schools—both public and parochial.

President Johnson delivered his education message calling for a new federal initiative in support of elementary and secondary education on January 12, 1965. The same day legislation to accomplish the president's goals was introduced in the House by Congressman Carl D. Perkins, a Kentucky Democrat and senior member of the Committee on Education and Labor. H.R. 2362, of which I was a cosponsor, moved quickly through the legislative labyrinth. Hearings began within two weeks; by March the full committee had approved a bill, which was cleared by the Rules Committee for floor consideration and passed by the full House on March 26—two months and two weeks after LBJ's message to Congress.

To speed the process, the Senate sponsors managed to approve a bill identical to the House version and thereby avoid a conference. A conference committee, which is composed of members of both the House and the Senate who have worked on a measure in their respective bodies, must reconcile any differences between the bills passed by the two chambers. And so on April 9—less than three months after its introduction—Congress approved the Elementary and Secondary Education Act of 1965.

ESEA began a new era in federal aid to education. In one stroke the federal share of elementary and secondary education expenditures was doubled. Programs to aid the educationally disadvantaged, provide instructional materials, support innovative measures in schools, improve research, and strengthen state education agencies were established by the new law. Although it was President Johnson who provided the initial thrust for this historic advance, it must be clear that without allies on the Hill his proposal would never have moved successfully through Congress. As Eidenberg and Morey observe, "The power to initiate congressional debate is not the power to direct the conclusions of that debate."[6]

The President's success with ESEA rested in large part on his political skills and those of his appointees in designing a bill that muted controversy and drew solid support from hitherto opposed factions. The measure was one that could be passed, and its unique and imaginative provisions rescued members of Congress from their basic fear of becoming embroiled once more in the bitter school-aid battles of the past.

EXECUTIVE-LEGISLATIVE INTERACTION: NIE AND THE INTERNATIONAL EDUCATION ACT

The case history of another measure with which I was involved illustrates an important variation on the "president proposes—Congress disposes" theme. For while it was true that the idea to create an institute for educational research sprang in 1970 from the White House, the impetus for the translation of the idea into law came from Congress. Declaring that "we are not getting as much as we should out of the dollars we spend on education," President Richard M. Nixon, in his education message to Congress of March 3, 1970, asked for the establishment of a National Institute of Education. Although I was a Democrat and had been hostile to Nixon since his first campaign for a seat in Congress against Jerry Voorhis in 1946, I thought the president's proposal highly constructive and decided to sponsor the bill to establish the institute.

I was very sympathetic to the idea of the NIE. In 1961, during my second term, Adam Clayton Powell, Jr., chairman of the Education and Labor Committee, created an Advisory Group on Higher Education and named me chairman. A major recommendation of our group was for "special attention to ways of fostering high-quality basic research on the learning process with a view to improving the effectiveness of teaching and learning at all levels." My own educational back-

[6] Ibid., p. 228.

ground, my experience as a teacher, my conversations with academics, my frustrations as a legislator seeking adequate information on which to base policy—all these factors confirmed me in the judgment that the National Institute of Education was an idea whose time had come. I saw my job, in the spring of 1970, as one of transforming a recommendation the White House had made halfheartedly into a legislative proposal of sufficient interest to win the support of my committee colleagues. I did so, and, as I explain in chapter 3, the National Institute of Education became law in 1972.

Navigating White House ideas through legislative seas is usually, of course, much easier when a member of Congress is dealing with a president of his own party. Here the International Education Act is illustrative. This measure, signed into law by President Johnson in 1966, authorized grants to colleges and universities in the United States for international studies and research at both the undergraduate and graduate levels. As with the NIE years later, I quickly expressed interest in a proposal voiced by President Johnson in 1965 and persuaded Chairman Powell to create a task force to handle the legislation and name me chairman. I shared Johnson's conviction that strengthening international studies at American universities was vital to the country, and I was, therefore, enthusiastic about writing the White House initiative into law—and won passage of the bill.

There are several points that these legislative examples underscore. First, it is not enough for a president to lay his ideas before Congress and then sit in the White House awaiting results. If a president's proposals are to become law, they must strike a responsive chord in legislators willing to sponsor and guide them through the obstacle course on Capitol Hill. The striking of such chords may result from a number of factors: a president's high standing in the polls (other things being equal, a popular president finds it easier to convince legislators of the correctness of his position); a lawmaker's desire to stake out for himself or herself an area of expertise; and a member's firmly held conviction that a problem exists and calls for the remedy proposed. None of these factors is mutually exclusive; often all are present at once, and any of them enhances congressional receptivity to presidential initiatives.

My second point is that, given the range of intangibles—personal prejudices, intellectual predispositions, even religious convictions—that governs the attitudes of congressmen toward ideas for policy, those observers who approach politics as a science must proceed cautiously. Rigid cause-and-effect models of congressional behavior, which posit presidents, constituents, or interest groups as acting on passive legislators to produce policy outcomes, can be misleading. Such constructs may obscure the role legislators themselves play and fail to take into account—because so difficult to quantify—the human variables of ambition, interests, and skill.

My final point is an obvious one: the examples of the Elementary and Secondary Education Act, the National Institute of Education, and the International Education Act demonstrate that, even when ideas for legislation emanate from elsewhere, it is often members of Congress who refine, shape, and mold the ideas into law.

CONGRESS AS LEGISLATIVE LEADER: THE MIDDLE INCOME STUDENT ASSISTANCE ACT

I turn now to a clear example of congressional initiative in education: the Middle Income Student Assistance Act of 1978. The trigger for this legislation was the rising sentiment in Congress in 1977 for a tuition tax-credit bill.[7] Two of us on the Education and Labor Committee who strongly opposed the tax-credit scheme, Democratic Congressman William D. Ford of Michigan and I, warned Joseph A. Califano, Jr., secretary

---

[7] In January, 1977, a bill was introduced by Senator William Roth (R.-Del.) to establish a tax credit for tuition paid to a college, university, or postsecondary vocational school. The Roth bill was cosponsored by Senators Daniel Patrick Moynihan (D.-N.Y.) and Robert Packwood (R.-Ore.), who broadened the credit to include tuition paid to private elementary and secondary schools.

of health, education, and welfare, of a political vacuum in the absence of a White House alternative to tax credits that would help families with college-bound students. "If Carter doesn't propose something, we will," we said.

Our disagreement with tuition tax credits stemmed from several considerations. First, we doubted the constitutionality of tax credits for parochial schools. Second, tuition tax credits entailed huge revenue losses, which would undoubtedly be described as "expenditures" for education, and in a federal budget of finite resources such "expenditures" would severely constrict funding for other education programs. Third, such a program, by diminishing available resources, would substantially weaken the nation's hard-pressed public schools. Finally, because the proposal involved taxes, it would bring the House Ways and Means Committee and the Senate Finance Committee into policymaking for education. We on the Education and Labor Committee did not look kindly at the prospect of sharing our authority in this area.

Beyond constitutional, financial, and jurisdictional apprehensions about tuition tax credits, my allies and I had another reason for advocating the Middle Income Assistance Act. We were increasingly sensitive to the fact that many American families, although not poor, were needy in terms of their capacity to afford a college education for their sons and daughters, especially families with several children in college.[8] We were therefore concerned about our middle-income constituents in our home districts.

Finally, as champions of financial assistance for students from poor families, who lacked the influence at the polls of middle-income voters, we realized that, by broadening the political base of support for federal student aid, we would help protect it for low-income students.

A few days after our meeting with Secretary Califano, Stuart Eizenstat, the president's domestic-policy chief, and Hale

[8]For examples drawn from New York University that illustrate this point, see chap. 6.

Champion, undersecretary of HEW, met with Ford and me in my House majority whip's office in the Capitol. "Bill and I have drafted a bill to extend aid to students who although from middle-income families need help to pay for college," I told the administration officials. "We have to have a bill to head off the tax credit. You can't beat something with nothing. Now this train [our bill] is pulling out of the station, and the only question for the president is whether or not he wants on board."

The president decided not only to buy a train ticket but to become the engineer. On February 8, 1978, Congressmen Carl Perkins, Frank Thompson (D.-N.J.), and Ford, Senator Claiborne Pell (D.-R.I.), and I stood alongside President Carter in the White House Press Room as he announced that *he* was proposing a Middle Income Student Assistance Bill. The president made it clear that he would not accept both it and the tuition tax credit.

After several months of contentious debate, both the House and the Senate approved what had become the Carter administration's student-aid bill, and the president signed it into law on November 1, 1978.

REFLECTIONS ON LEGISLATIVE LEADERSHIP

Any bill passed by Congress is a tapestry woven from strands of intellectual effort, political opportunity, institutional rivalry, and personal ambition. When the threads of influence are untangled and the complexities and nuances of the process are sifted, Congress emerges as a major source of ideas for policy. Even in those instances when the proposals are first conceived outside the legislative arena, the record of the bills I have discussed makes clear that members of Congress often play a seminal role in translating new concepts into proposals that eventually become law.

Both the possibilities of and the limits on Congress as an engine of policy leadership flow from its basic nature as (1) a representative body of 535 individuals compelled to forge and sustain state and district ties and to face, at two- and six-year intervals, periodic elections at times certain and (2) a decision-making body that acts through bargaining and consensus to build coalitions to effect changes in public policy for the nation.

Let me linger on these dual roles.[9] Congressmen and senators are representative of local districts or states and, therefore, must be sensitive to local and state feelings about national policy and its administration. Our legislators in Washington in effect serve as links between locally perceived needs and the formulation and implementation of national policy. That lawmakers are elected rather than appointed is of course fundamental to their ability to be genuine representatives.

Senators and congressmen are also national legislators; the bills they pass apply to the entire country, not just their constituencies. The kinds of issues with which the American government must deal today require coherent policies for 230 million people living in fifty states and the territories.

Senators and congressmen develop unusual skill as brokers among private individuals and groups and officials at every level of government, local, state and federal. Congressional politicians are nurtured in negotiation; they swim in a pluralistic sea. Bargaining among disparate forces is their natural way of life.

Several propositions flow from these basic tenets of congressional life and bear on the role of the legislature as a source and shaper of ideas for policy:

1. It is simply not possible, given the limits of human intelligence, for the executive branch to be the sole source of thinking; certainly the executive alone is unable to transform worthwhile ideas into public policy. Nor, for that matter, is there really a single executive; there are many executives, and

[9]For the following analysis I have drawn, in part, on an earlier essay of mine, "Congress in the Year 2000," in Harvey Perloff, ed., The Future of the United States Government (New York: George Brazillier, 1970).

some are less open to innovation than others. In any event, like the elected president, Congress is politically hypersensitive, always looking toward the next election and eager to cultivate measures to command public attention and approbation.

As we have seen, Congress has the capacity, independent of the executive, to be a source and advocate of policy alternatives—a function of great value to the executive and the nation, on the reasonable assumption that a complex and changing society like ours will be in constant need of new ideas.

2. Not only the executive but the legislative branch can catapult ideas into public view, give them visibility, and clothe them with the respectability essential to serious consideration by a public much broader than the group that spawned them. But the two branches launch ideas in different ways. The executive proposes policy by promulgating a legislative program. Crucial executive debate on alternatives, however, takes place for the most part internally and privately. Not only does the executive fail to call attention to the full range of possible actions, but often it resents public reports that debate is taking place. For the executive does not wish to cultivate a public garden of all possibilities; it seeks to assemble a bouquet to be offered as the best of all prospects. The result is to contract the field of visible options.

In contrast, the natural operation of Congress expands the range of alternatives. Through this constant search for a vehicle with which to win public attention, every member of Congress becomes an instrument by which ideas can be propelled into public view. Ideas can attach themselves to individual members, committees, party organizations, and informal groups of members. By introducing bills, holding hearings, giving speeches, and conducting floor debates, members can discern, stimulate, and capture the interest of the public.

All these activities of Congress make it possible for public policy to be welcomed, accepted, or at least tolerated by the citizenry. Congressional involvement, moreover, given the multiplicity of views expressed and the visible nature of many proceedings, is at least as likely to produce intelligent policy as could be generated by the executive acting alone. As James Sundquist asserts, the American system derives "its unique vitality" from its "multiple centers of legislative initiative." [10]

3. One may complain that the dual legislative process often makes it difficult for government to act decisively. The response to this contention must be somewhat complicated. The Constitution itself, prescribing separated powers and mandating checks and balances, when coupled with the diversity of American society, is not ideally tailored for decisive governmental action. Nor, indeed, is the voice with which the American voter speaks always decisive, as the last several years, in which the White House and Senate have been controlled by one party and the House of Representatives by another, attest. Our government, for better or for worse, does not seem so ill-matched to the nature of our society.

Moreover, those who complain about congressional obstruction of presidential proposals often fail to acknowledge that Congress can block presidential initiatives that better judgment decrees are not sound. This is not a difficult observation for a former Democratic congressman writing in 1986 to voice.

4. The conditions of legislative life put a premium on leadership as bargaining. The skillful building of coalitions in Congress requires patience, diligence, and sensitivity to the constraints under which one's colleagues operate. Those constraints may include constituent or interest-group pressures, appeals from party leaders, and calls to conscience.

Whereas the president, through superior access to the media, can command center stage to project his policies directly and dramatically to the public, a legislator labors less visibly—

[10]Sundquist, *Politics and Policy*, p. 535.

and often deliberately so. At times part of the lawmaker's task must be to obscure the importance of a policy change, to downplay its impact, so as to keep legislative options open as long as possible and thereby enhance the chances of passage.

In sum, then, the structure and dynamics of Congress dictate that for our first branch of government the process of policy initiation will be (1) porous, open to myriad influences—constituent, interest group, presidential, and media; (2) uneven, developed in fits and starts; and (3) messy, entangled with the political agendas and timetables of hundreds of individually elected representatives and senators. But the fact remains that Congress acts as both incubator and facilitator of public policies in America. The next step in the legislative process, the transition from generating ideas to writing laws, forms the topic of the following chapter.

CHAPTER 3

PATTERNS OF
CONGRESSIONAL POLICYMAKING

THERE ARE SEVERAL DIMENSIONS to policymaking: the setting of agendas; the shaping of bills and resolutions; the development and implementation of programs to carry out the intent of legislation; and the review and evaluation of those programs once established. Chapter 2 focused on the first of these dimensions: the means by which ideas for policy are injected into the legislative arena. In this chapter I explore the dynamics of decision making: the strategies and maneuvers that underlie the textbook description of "how a bill becomes a law." In addition, I discuss the relationship of legislators to their constituents, to the federal bureaucracy, and to the president; and I review the responsibilities of Congress to oversee the results in practice of the proposals that reach the statute books.

FORGING A BILL

Students of the way federal education policy is made and the role of Congress in its formation will find few cases more illuminating than the Education Amendments of 1972. From the National Defense Education Act of 1958 under Dwight Eisenhower to the Higher Education Facilities Act of 1963—proposed by John Kennedy and enacted under Lyndon Johnson—to the Higher Education Act of 1965, with its pioneering Educational Opportunity Grants for needy students, most initiatives for higher education policy came from the White House.

The presidency of Richard Nixon, however, signaled a significantly different configuration of political forces in Washington, and like other fields of policy, higher education was dramatically affected by the sharp change of environment. The Nixon years have been characterized by one political scientist as a period of "clashing institutional objectives" during which "the President proposed comparatively little substantive legislation, and his rate of success with the measures he supported was very low. Congress, on the other hand, initiated major new programs, frequently provoking Presidential vetoes."[1]

Senators and congressmen moved swiftly into the policy void Nixon left. In the Senate, Claiborne Pell (D.-R.I.), who in 1969 had assumed the chairmanship of the Education Subcommittee of the Labor and Public Welfare Committee,[2] worked to devise a form of financial assistance that would go directly to college students. By the summer of 1971, Pell's proposal was crystallized into "Basic Educational Opportunity Grants" for needy students during their undergraduate years. A bill that included these grants, along with a range of other higher edu-

---

[1] Gary Orfield, *Congressional Power: Congress and Social Change* (New York: Harcourt Brace Jovanovich, 1975), pp. 5–6. Orfield adds, "Assuming office after an indecisive election where the Presidential vote was split three ways, Mr. Nixon brought with him to Washington virtually no social program except a pledge to slow down civil rights enforcement and become tougher on crime." P. 55. "He [Nixon] vetoed urban and environmental measures; bills to promote education, job creation, campaign reform, and health care." P. 56. Between 1969, when he took office, and 1974, when he resigned, Nixon vetoed 41 bills, 5 of which were overridden. In a fascinating account of executive-legislative relations during the Nixon era, Charles O. Jones observes that Nixon came to office with "negative evaluations" of both the "legitimacy" and "competency" of Congress and had decided the country could be better run without it. "This conclusion of Nixon's was facilitated by his priorities— foreign policy and the reduction of domestic programs. Had Nixon wished to enact an elaborate domestic program, he would have been less free to exclude Congress." Charles O. Jones, "Congress and the Presidency," in Thomas E. Mann and Norman J. Ornstein, eds., *The New Congress* (Washington, D.C.: American Enterprise Institute, 1981), pp. 231–32.

[2] Now the Labor and Human Resources Committee.

cation initiatives, was approved unanimously by the Senate Labor and Public Welfare committee and passed by the full Senate on August 6, 1971.

The ease with which the senators acted was not emulated in the House. Hearings conducted by Edith Green (D.-Ore.), chairman of the Special Education Subcommittee of the Education and Labor Committee, on a bill she had drafted in consultation with the higher education interest groups marked the start of a highly controversial struggle that was to last for four years.

A former public schoolteacher, Mrs. Green was at the time the member of the House of Representatives most closely identified with education. She was especially proud of her role as an advocate of higher education, a field in which, in an appraisal widely shared, "she typically displayed an impressive, unmatched command of the legislation."[3] Her relations with other members of the Education and Labor Committee, however, became increasingly strained, and the late 1960s saw a growing rift between Mrs. Green and her committee colleagues, including me.[4] I had, for example, led the opposition to a bill Mrs. Green introduced in early 1969 to cut off all federal aid to colleges that had experienced student unrest. The fight was intense, bitter, and bipartisan.

The Nixon administration, speaking through Secretary of Health, Education, and Welfare Robert Finch, also opposed the Green bill on grounds that it represented improper intervention by the federal government into matters that should be

[3]Lawrence E. Gladieux and Thomas R. Wolanin, *Congress and the Colleges* (Lexington, Mass.: Lexington Books, 1976), p. 83. This book is an insightful, informative, and highly readable account of the legislative history surrounding the Education Amendments of 1972.

[4]An illustration of this tension is found in a memorandum to President Lyndon Johnson from Douglass Cater, a White House assistant on education matters. The memo, on White House stationery and dated March 30, 1965, speaks for itself:
"TO: THE PRESIDENT
FR: Douglass Cater
Adam Clayton Powell is burning mad over Edith Green's behavior on the

controlled by local and state authorities. The Green bill was defeated in subcommittee and then in full committee by a dramatic vote of 18 to 17.

Although earlier in her congressional career Mrs. Green had won a reputation as a champion of civil rights and school integration, by the late 1960s she had become one of the most influential allies of the southern conservatives and an insistent proponent of antibusing measures. Beyond our ideological disagreements, I found my conflicts with this highly intelligent and forceful fellow Democrat exacerbated by differences in personal and legislative styles and a competitiveness that can arise at times between two legislators interested in making their reputation in the same area.

Indeed, so hostile to me had Mrs. Green become that in January, 1971, in the early days of the Ninety-first Congress, she attempted to change the rules of the Committee on Education and Labor for the sole purpose of denying me a seat on the Higher Education Subcommittee she chaired. Although her effort failed, I did not take it as a constructive contribution to the quality of our relationship. Our personal and philosophical differences were later to prove significant in the shaping of federal policy for education.

As we began to write the higher education provisions of what in 1972 became law, Congress reached out to many sources for ideas—to foundations, commissions, university presidents, and research institutes as well as staff in the administration. What is essential to assert here is that in producing the higher-education titles of this measure the fundamental decisions were made by a few senators and congressmen influenced by the work of a nongovernmental commission and two or three experts whose views we respected. Both the executive branch and the higher-education interest groups proved essentially irrelevant to the result.

Despite Nixon's apathy toward higher education, Claiborne Pell in the Senate moved ahead on his plan for grants to students, while in the House Mrs. Green pushed hard for her proposal for general aid to colleges and universities, so-called institutional aid. Much influenced by reports of a "new depression in higher education,"[5] she worked closely with the higher education groups to fashion a bill to provide grants to colleges and universities based on their enrollments. It should be noted that the Green formula, in employing this "capitation" (i.e., per student) approach, did not take into account the *need* of an institution for assistance. There was no provision to link the amount of aid provided to the financial strength of a college or university; there was, in this sense, a complete lack of discrimination among institutions.

Neither Mrs. Green nor the representatives of colleges and universities and the higher education associations brought other members of her subcommittee, of whom I was next senior Democrat, into their negotiations.[6] Given that in 1969, at considerable political risk to myself, I had worked diligently—and effectively—to kill the Green campus-unrest bill that the college and university community so much feared, I was not amused that, in the development of new proposals for aid to higher education, its principal representatives in Washington, D.C., turned their backs on me to put all their eggs in Mrs. Green's basket.

But beyond this source of irritation, I was much more concerned about what I believed to have been the failure of the American university community as a whole to give serious, systematic thought to the question of federal "institutional

---

Education Bill. He has threatened three reprisals:
1. Remove vocational rehabilitation from her Subcommittee jurisdiction.
2. Fire her sister from the Committee staff.
3. Entrust John Brademas with sponsorship of the Higher Education Bill. Brademas is uncertain about No. 3, but is willing to undertake the job if it will serve the good of the Bill."
The president's hand-scribbled response was succinct: "O.K. all 3."

[5] The phrase is from the title of one of the most influential documents in the debate over aid to colleges and universities, Earl F. Cheit's *The New Depression in Higher Education: A General Report for the Carnegie Commission on Higher Education and the Ford Foundation* (New York: McGraw-Hill, 1970).

[6] According to Gladieux and Wolanin, the alliance of Mrs. Green and the

aid" to colleges and universities. At a breakfast in the House Dining Room with the chief lobbyist for higher education, a highly respected individual (and a former member of Mrs. Green's subcommittee staff), I pressed him for some rational justification of an aid formula that would have given just as much federal money per student to Harvard University, with its huge endowment, as to Boston University, just across the Charles River, with a far smaller endowment. "That formula makes no sense," I argued. "How can you possibly justify it?"

"Because," came the reply, "we"—meaning the higher-education interest groups—"agree on it." I told the spokesman that *I* did not agree with either the formula or its rationale and that I had expected from the nation's citadels of reason more thoughtful, objective arguments in support of federal policy toward colleges and universities.[7]

When Mrs. Green began hearings in 1969, two bills were before the subcommittee: her own, which based aid to institutions on student head counts, and one that I, together with Ogden Reid (R.-N.Y.), had introduced, which was inspired by recommendations of the Carnegie Commission on Higher Education.[8] The Brademas-Reid Bill rejected the pleas of the

---

asociations was based on policy agreement (". . . for several years higher education had supported institutional aid to relieve the financial pinch"); convenience ("Having once reached consensus, there was a strong pressure against reopening old wounds"); and pressure from Mrs. Green (". . . whose personality and political style required strict loyalty from her allies"). Gladieux and Wolanin, *Congress and the Colleges*, pp. 130–31.

[7]This experience later helped persuade me strongly to support an initiative of Congressman James Scheuer (D.-N.Y.) to create a National Commission on Financing Postsecondary Education. The NCFPSE, authorized in the 1972 Education Amendments, undertook the task of devising an analytical framework within which legislators, university leaders and others responsible for making policy to finance higher education could more carefully and systematically consider options and alternatives. The commission, on which I served, produced a report in 1974 entitled *Financing Postsecondary Education in the United States*, which I believe still merits attention.

[8]In 1967 the Carnegie Foundation, looking toward the year 2000, created a prestigious 15-member Commission on Higher Education to study and make recommendations on issues facing higher education. The first commission re-

higher education lobby to tie institutional aid to enrollments and proposed instead to link it to the cost of instructing students. Reid and I reasoned that because a college or university spent more to educate a student than he or she normally paid in tuition and fees, where a student's enrollment was, in part, made possible by federal aid that he or she received, the federal government should help pay part of the increased burden of instruction.

At this point another important congressional actor must be introduced, Congressman Albert M. Quie of Minnesota, with whom I had worked closely on several matters since my first years of service on the Education and Labor Committee. A Republican, a farmer, deeply religious, highly intelligent, Quie was a tough negotiator but pragmatic in outlook and, on the issues with which he and I wrestled, usually moderate in his approach. We were both strongly committed to higher education and especially concerned about the state of private colleges and universities. Although each of us was at times a vigorous partisan, we both saw mutual advantage in forging bipartisan agreements wherever we could. For Quie the opportunity to join forces with a Democrat who was a senior on the committee considerably enhanced his influence, while for my part an alliance with a respected Republican who could bring votes both in committee and in the House significantly strengthened my hand. With a Republican in the White House who was likely to be hostile to whatever legislation we drafted, a coalition with Quie was especially helpful. Quie's vocal support would cause Nixon to think twice before vetoing a bill:

port, *Quality and Equality: New Levels of Federal Responsibility for Higher Education,* was issued in late 1968 and called for a significant expansion of federal funds for aid to students. One recommendation was for a new program of direct assistance to institutions based on a "cost-of-instruction" formula under which colleges and universities would receive federal funds based on the numbers of enrolled students *holding federal grants.* The rationale for this formula was that the federal government should reimburse an institution for a portion of the additional costs it incurred in admitting federally aided students.

the Minnesotan could bring along enough Republicans to override a veto.

Quie became more and more fearful that the Green across-the-board proposal for institutional aid would favor the rich institutions, and he and I, joined by Congressmen Frank Thompson (D.-N.J.) and John Dellenback (R.-Ore), quietly began seeking an alternative on which the four of us could agree.

In August, 1971, the Senate passed, without much controversy or fanfare, its version of a higher-education bill,[9] the centerpiece of which was Pell's basic grants to students.[10] The House came under increasing pressure to act. By this time the bills on both sides of Capitol Hill were evolving into omnibus measures, each carrying several legislative "passengers" brought on board by various committee members. One such passenger in the House was my National Institute of Education.

As finally reported by the committee, the House measure contained an institutional-aid compromise that Green successfully defended on the House floor. But the voting there in the fall of 1971 added new dimensions to the story. Although as a committee member I faithfully supported Green in voting against floor amendments to eliminate her institutional-aid provision, about which I had my reservations, and also voted against adding to the bill the Pell Grants, which in principle I favored, she spoke vigorously in support of an amendment to kill the one title of the bill that was my handiwork, the National Institute of Education. Only votes from the Republican side preserved the NIE. Green's open opposition to the NIE despite my support of her bill marked a dividing point in my relationship with her; she had no reason to expect my further cooperation in the House-Senate conference on the legislation.

[9] Barely mustering a quorum before the beginning of the summer recess, the Senate passed the higher-education bill, S. 659, by a roll call vote of 51-0.
[10] The basic-grant entitlement was set at $1,200 less the amount a family could be expected to contribute toward their child's college education.

I took part in many conferences during twenty-two years in Congress, but none so lengthy, difficult, or fascinating—and ultimately gratifying—as that on the Education Amendments of 1972. Beginning in March of that year and continuing for nine weeks, congressmen and senators—including, among others, Edward M. Kennedy (D.-Mass.), Walter F. Mondale (D.-Minn.), Thomas F. Eagleton (D.-Mo.), Alan Cranston (D.-Cal.), Jacob K. Javits (R.-N.Y.), and Claiborne Pell (D.-R.I.)— met in room S207 on the Senate side of the Capitol. It was a room with which I was to become familiar. A simple yet stately chamber added to the Senate wing of the Capitol barely a dozen years before, S207 had walls of dark, carved wood, bare except for a Gilbert Stuart portrait of George Washington hanging above the white-marble mantle and gazing out over the conferees at work.

My major objective—and that of Quie and our allies—was to win enough votes among the other House conferees to be able to agree to the Senate provisions both on the Pell Basic Grants and on institutional aid. On both items we preferred the Senate language. Carl Perkins, who had served in the House since 1948 and since 1967 had been chairman of the Education and Labor Committee, was a tall, constantly smiling man from the hollows of Kentucky whose concern for the well-being of his low-income constituents made him an ardent advocate of federal social programs, including education.[11] He was a strong liberal in his views, and his country twang and self-effacing demeanor concealed superb political skill. Claiborne Pell, patrician descendant of a prominent New England family, former Foreign Service officer, and one of the wealthiest members of the Senate, was Perkins's counterpart

[11] Carl Perkins's death in August, 1984, was deeply lamented by those of us who had worked with him in his pursuit of social justice and equal opportunity for all Americans. It is reassuring, however, to see the name Perkins among the members of the House of Representatives on the Education and Labor Committee. Chris Perkins, chosen in a special election in 1984 to represent Kentucky's Seventh District, follows in the footsteps of his distinguished father.

as chairman of the Senate conferees. The two men embodied two important traditions in the national Democratic party. Despite differences in background, they were both progressive in outlook, intent on expanding educational opportunity, and determined, in the parlance of the Hill, "to get a bill."

Pell's major goal was, of course, his Basic Grant. Quie and I favored some version of that as well as the new program of aid to colleges and universities. Chairman Perkins became our covert ally after a speech Mrs. Green made on the House floor in which she sharply attacked the House conferees for our decisions in conference up to that point and predicted that agreement on any bill was unlikely. An indignant Perkins gave me authority to resolve the remaining student-grant and institutional-aid issues. My staff assistant, James P. Mooney, and I drafted a compromise formula to which Pell and his Senate colleagues privately agreed.

With Perkins in our camp, Quie and I knew that we had reached an accord on the questions most important to us. All parties to the understanding on institutional aid resolved to keep it secret. Early in the morning of May 17, 1972, after the conferees had resolved the extraneous but highly contentious issue of school busing, Senator Pell and I, as if by prearrangement—which was the case!—exchanged an offer and counteroffer on the institutional-aid formula that we had earlier written. On the question of how the federal government should provide general assistance to colleges and universities,[12] Mrs. Green had lost. The conference adjourned at 5:13 A.M., and the conferees, exhausted but exhilarated by our achievement, stumbled out into the dawn on the Capitol steps.

When I say "our" achievement, I refer to the senators, the congressmen, and our staffs, for on the key provisions of the

[12] Not long afterward, in January, 1973, Mrs. Green relinquished her chairmanship of the Higher Education Subcommittee (and almost two decades of seniority) for a seat on the Appropriations Committee. Gladieux and Wolanin speculate that her move was born of her frustration over her defeat on the higher education bill. She retired from the House the following year.

Education Amendments of 1972, neither representatives of the administration nor those of the higher-education interest groups had played significant roles. The House of Representatives approved the conference agreement on June 8, 1972, nearly four years after Mrs. Green's first hearings on her higher education bill.

The measure we wrote was an important step in the evolving role of the federal government in higher education. The new law fixed firmly among our national commitments the principle that an opportunity for a college education should be denied no talented and motivated student because of financial need.

Ironically, the issue of student aid was often obscured in the swirling, highly emotional debates that surrounded school busing and campus unrest. One further irony: despite the months of struggle to produce an institutional-aid program, Congress never appropriated any money to implement it, and in subsequent years institutional aid faded as an issue. For higher education the lasting legacy of 1972 was what came to be known as the Pell Grants for students.

DECIDING WHO GETS WHAT

We have seen how the shaping of a significant higher-education measure turned in large part on the question of what formula to use for distributing federal funds to colleges and universities. In 1973 and 1974 I was again embroiled in a contest over allocation of money, this time for Title I of the Elementary and Secondary Education Act. This battle, precipitated by the release of new census data, pitted congressmen from the large, industrial states against those from the smaller, rural ones.[13] Not long after, in working on legislation to help states

[13]Title I (now Chapter 1) of the Elementary and Secondary Education Act provides assistance to local school districts to help disadvantaged and minority students. The original formula established in 1965 to distribute Title I funds took into account two factors: the number of poor children in a school district and the per pupil expenditure by the state. To arrive at an estimate of

pay for educating handicapped children, I again devoted considerable energy to working out equations for deciding how much money went to each state.

Time and again during consideration of legislation on federal aid to education, the most intense warfare involved issues of rules and eligibility, allocation formulas, and definitions of need. Centering on measurements of income, per pupil expenditures, and cost of instruction, these matters were often highly technical and complex. They nonetheless entailed some of the basic controversies in politics: who is to get how much money, by what rules the money is to be allocated, and for what purpose it is to be spent.

Although complicated and often tedious to follow, fights on formulas offer revealing lessons about the policy process. First, members usually cast their votes on such issues not according to ideology but to protect the interests of their districts. The battles are intense precisely because they involve bringing home the bacon to one's constituents.

Second, in the arena of lawmaking, the force of individual personality still looms large. In 1973, when the Title I reformulation was being considered, the industrial states dominated the House Education Committee. But the tenacity of Chairman Perkins in defending the concerns of his Kentucky constituents caused an impasse in the committee that led to an eventual compromise more favorable to the rural states. In

---

the number of poor children in a district, Congress decided to use, from the latest decennial census, the number of families below an annual income level of $2,000 and the number of families receiving Aid to Families with Dependent Children (AFDC) payments in excess of $2,000 a year. This formula was in effect from 1965 to 1973. In 1973, however, when the 1970 decennial census was automatically applied to the formula, Title I funds declined dramatically in poor rural states while rising in big industrial states. These results were essentially due to the combination, between 1960 and 1970, of a steep drop in the number of families with incomes below $2,000 and a steady growth in the number of AFDC families. The chief battleground for the dispute over changing the formula in 1973 was the House Education and Labor Committee. The struggle was especially complicated because members from the large industrial states, which benefited from the new census, dominated the committee,

1974 I was able, at Perkins's request, to take the lead in breaking the deadlock in large part because in the rival formulas, my state—Indiana—would neither lose much nor gain much.[14] My credibility on the issue was high.

Third, once a compromise is reached on a difficult matter, members are extremely reluctant to tamper further for fear that a carefully stitched together accommodation will unravel. The so-called Brademas formula for Title I funds survived committee and floor action in both House and Senate in 1973 and, with only a minor modification, is still the law of the land.

MEETING OPPOSITION

Obviously not every idea a Congressman has is translated into a federal statute. Very few ideas become bills, and very few bills become laws.[15] Although I was successful with a number of proposals, I had my share of defeats. Legislation in the area of early childhood development is one example.

Having been actively involved in the shaping of the Head Start program,[16] I decided in 1969, when I became chairman of

while members from rural states were in the minority. Chairman Perkins represented a state that lost funds under the formula.

[14] After a five-month debate the compromise "Brademas formula" was accepted by the committee on January 30, 1974, by a vote of 23-8. The compromise permitted the new 1970 census data to take effect but with these changes: the definition of poverty was updated from $2,000 a year to $3,743 a year; the gains of the large states were moderated by changing the maximum payment per eligible child from 50 percent of the greater of the state or national average per pupil expenditure to 40 percent of the state average, with a floor of 80 percent and a ceiling of 120 percent of the national average; only two-thirds of the children in families receiving AFDC payments above the annual poverty income level for a nonfarm family of four would be included in the formula. I include this description not to baffle the reader but to convey some sense of the complexity of formulas when the political stakes are high. The Brademas formula was eventually approved by the full House and accepted by the Senate.

[15] For example, in the Ninety-eighth Congress (1983–84), of 12,798 bills introduced over the two-year period, only 677 were enacted into law.

[16] Enacted in 1965, the Head Start program was designed to address the educational, health, and nutritional needs of economically disadvantaged

the Select Education Subcommittee, to draft legislation that would offer opportunities for other than poor families for pre-natal care, day care, and related services.[17] I did so and next found a Senate cosponsor, the then junior senator from Minnesota, Walter F. Mondale. After Mondale and I conducted many days of hearings over a three-year period, we saw that so wide a consensus had been developed on the need for child-care services and on approaches to provide them that by 1971 a revised version of our bill was being cosponsored by more than one hundred members of the House of both parties.

The major obstacle to the legislation came not from the Nixon administration or congressional Republicans but from a man with whom in every other fight I had found myself allied, Carl D. Perkins, chairman of the committee. Representing a district in Kentucky with few towns of even medium size, Perkins vigorously opposed a provision in the bill setting 100,000 as the minimum population required for a community to sponsor a child-care program. Perkins was adamant on the point, and although the Committee on Education and Labor voted to report the bill, he prevented it from being considered on the House floor.

Perkins's hostility was the reason I felt compelled, months later, in the fall of 1971, to offer my bill—as reported by the full Committee on Education and Labor—as an amendment to separate legislation on the floor. I prevailed; the House

---

children aged three through five. Head Start remains one of the most successful achievements of the Great Society.

[17] Seventeen years later the problem that concerned my colleagues and me has only grown worse. There are today 16.2 million working women with children under the age of thirteen; more than half of all children under the age of six have mothers in the work force. Clearly it is now the rule and not the exception for mothers of preschoolers to work outside the home. The issue has attracted renewed attention in Congress as well as the media. In 1983 the House of Representatives established a Select Committee on Children, Youth, and Families which, under the able leadership of Congressman George Miller (D.-Calif.), has been studying public policy options for family and child services. Several legislative proposals for day-care assistance have been introduced in the present House and Senate.

voted to accept the Brademas initiative on child care.[18] House Minority Leader Gerald R. Ford attempted, on a subsequent motion, to eliminate my amendment. It survived—barely—by a vote of 186 to 183.

Naturally I was elated, but my joy was short-lived. So unhappy with my victory was Perkins that, despite my having been chief author of what had become a major title of the bill, he denied me appointment as one of the House conferees to meet with our Senate counterparts on the legislation. I was enraged and told Perkins so. Although clearly embarrassed, he continued to exclude me. Not surprisingly, the final version of the legislation contained Perkins's lower minimum population requirement—five thousand—to accommodate smaller and rural communities. On this provision Perkins had triumphed over me.[19]

This incident marked the only such encounter with Perkins that I had during twenty-two years on the committee. I remained his ally, aware that few legislators had contributed so much to American education as he. I cite the event because it demonstrates how constituency interest can deeply—I do not say improperly—affect policy decisions in Congress.[20] The incident also shows how legislative warfare can occur within the same party and between friends.

[18]The vehicle I used for my child-care initiative was legislation to extend the life of the Office of Economic Opportunity, the lead agency of the antipoverty program.

[19]Not until 1974 did the full Congress approve a Child Development Bill, and it was vetoed by President Nixon. The fate of a similar measure introduced by Senator Mondale and me the following year provides an ironic commentary on attitudes toward children. Let me only note here that an extraordinary smear campaign was mounted against the legislation and against Senator Mondale and me. He and I had in fact already decided, for other reasons, to set our proposals aside. In what is known as a "committee print," the staff of my Select Education Subcommittee collected a sample of the scurrilous materials published in opposition to the bill and our responses to the attacks. See *Background Materials Concerning Child and Family Services Act, 1975,* H.R. 2966, 94th Cong., 2d sess. (December, 1976).

[20]By design and in practice Congress is preeminently a representative body.

OVERSEEING THE BUREAUCRACY

One of the most important responsibilities of Congress is oversight, i.e., inquiry into the implementation by the executive branch of legislation that Congress has passed and the President has signed. Although effective oversight requires time and energy, it can be a powerful instrument both to monitor the actions of the administration in office and to shed public light on significant problems.

I shall cite here three examples of oversight activity by my education subcommittee during three different administrations—those of Presidents Nixon, Ford, and Carter—but all in the same area: vocational rehabilitation of handicapped persons.

It is not easy today to recall the deepening hostility between the White House and Congress that characterized the year immediately following President Nixon's landslide victory in 1972. Beyond repeatedly resorting to the veto—twice of rehabilitation bills—Nixon again and again impounded monies appropriated by Congress for programs authorized by law. Confrontation was the order of the day. It was in such an environment that on August 3, 1973, my Select Education Subcommittee opened hearings to examine the administration of the vocational-rehabilitation program.

In looking back over the transcripts, I am reminded that I conducted the hearing as if I were a prosecuting attorney. First, I established that neither of the top officials in the Department of Health, Education, and Welfare with responsibility for rehabilitation had any experience in the field and then proceeded to reveal, in dramatic fashion, the contents of an internal memorandum that had been leaked to me. Written by the assistant secretary who that day was appearing before

---

Members of the House and Senate need not and should not display absolute fealty to the wishes of their constituents, but neither can they ignore them.

the subcommittee, the document recommended dismantling the historic vocational-rehabilitation program.

My indictment of the administration representatives was that they, first, had adduced no evidence to justify so radical a change in a program they had publicly conceded was effective, second, were unable to estimate the universe of need for rehabilitation services, and, third, had not been telling the subcommittee the truth.

The hearing produced an outpouring of protest, chiefly in the form of letters, by leaders in the vocational-rehabilitation community, both professionals in the field and representatives of handicapped advocates' groups. The changes the administration was contemplating were effectively smothered.

It was in a greatly changed atmosphere—Richard Nixon was no longer President; Gerald Ford was—that on December 10, 1975, I opened oversight hearings on extending the much-beleaguered Rehabilitation Act. This time the focus was on the use of federal funds by the states, specifically the request of Florida for a waiver of the provision of the law requiring each state to maintain a separate agency responsible for the handicapped program.

In this instance the hearing provided a forum for my colleagues and me to object strongly to pressure from Florida state officials for such a waiver. Our concern was that, if the political leaders of one state were permitted to dip into the federal monies expressly earmarked for the handicapped (90 percent federal–10 percent state was the match in the vocational-rehabilitation program) and to divert them to purposes unrelated to needs of the handicapped, still more states would clamor for the same opportunity, and a program expressly targeted to assist handicapped persons would be seriously weakened.

The clash between the state of Florida and organizations championing the disabled continued over several years, and the controversy ultimately spilled over into the courts. Not winning the waiver it sought from Congress, Florida sued the

Department of Health, Education, and Welfare. The U.S. Supreme Court resolved the issue on April 30, 1979, in *Florida Department of Health* v. *Joseph A. Califano, Jr., et al.* by reaffirming a lower-court ruling upholding the position my colleagues and I had maintained all along.

The third instance in which my subcommittee engaged in oversight on rehabilitation occurred early in President Carter's administration and dealt with one of his proposals for reorganization of the executive branch. The president's plan called for restructuring the Office of Human Development in what was then the Department of Health, Education, and Welfare. This office, with an annual budget of nearly $5 billion, administered a range of programs for handicapped persons, children, families, the elderly, and veterans.

When an assistant secretary of HEW testified before my subcommittee, the session was stormy. My colleagues and I were sharply critical of the reorganization for two reasons: (1) the administration had made no substantive case that the proposed changes would either improve services or save money; and (2) the administration had failed to consult either the constituent groups affected by the plan or those of us in Congress with legislative responsibility.

The administration simply asserted that its reorganization would be more efficient. In fact, the new table of organization was a political act—not in the partisan sense—after all, I was a Democrat attacking the proposal of a Democratic administration—but "political" in the sense that every reorganization means a redistribution of power and influence over policy. The reaction of my subcommittee colleagues and me, both Democrats and Republicans, to the assistant secretary's proposed changes was, to reiterate, hostile. The changes did not take place.

I cite these instances of congressional history because they dramatize the institutional imperative that often drives legislators. Over the span of four years, and through three administrations of both parties, I sought, as a member of the legislative branch, to protect programs I had helped create by means of critical scrutiny of their administration by the executive branch. The impulse for such confrontation is, of course, contained in the basic design of our national government and consists, as James Madison wrote in *The Federalist Papers,* "in giving to those who adminster each department the necessary constitutional means and personal motives to resist encroachments of others. . . . Ambition must be made to counteract ambition."

DEALING WITH THE WHITE HOUSE

The pattern and style of executive-congressional relations vary with the personality of the occupant of the White House, with the constellation of political forces, and with the particular issues. My relations with Presidents Kennedy and Johnson were, not surprisingly, more personal and friendly than those with Nixon. From the outset of his administration Kennedy worked hard to forge ties with lawmakers by inviting us to the White House in small groups for conversation and exchange of political intelligence. Johnson fashioned legislative victories out of personal loyalties, political obligations, and application of the famous "Johnson treatment."

For example, during consideration of the Elementary and Secondary Education Bill in my committee in the House, in 1965, I recall being present at a reception at the White House when Johnson took me aside to say, "Johnny,[21] I know what you're doing for me up there, and I appreciate it." The Johnson touch extended to his telephoning me to offer congratulations on my birthday. Such overtures leave a vivid imprint in the mind of a young congressman, and it is through such simple gestures that a president can build support—or at least ensure a sympathetic audience—on Capitol Hill.

By contrast, during the fight over the National Institute of Education, a White House initiative of which I was chief advo-

---

[21] President Johnson is the only person ever to call me "Johnny!"

cate in Congress, I had no contact at all with President Nixon or his staff.

Another, more recent example of dealing with the White House occurred while Jimmy Carter was president. In 1978, President Carter was not happy about a bill of mine to create White House Conferences on the Arts and Humanities. After first endorsing the legislation, the president sought to pull away from his commitment. A White House aide telephoned me to say that unless I agreed to amend the bill in certain ways the president would veto it.

Beyond the fact that my bill was a minor one, involving little money and that I disagreed on substantive grounds with the changes the president wanted, I was offended that he would go back on his word. Moreover, I was part of the House leadership, the majority whip, on whom the president depended to round up votes in support of legislation he was pressing. His attitude made little sense to me.

"That's not the way we do business around here," I said to the assistant. "If the president vetoes the bill, I'll make a speech on the House floor attacking him for breaking his promise." Even as the White House had prepared two statements for the president, one for a veto and the other for approval, so I had written two news releases, one to praise the president if he signed my bill, the other to criticize him if he vetoed it.

Carter did sign the bill, and I issued the release hailing his good judgment. As a postscript, I should note that no money was ever appropriated for the conferences, and they were never held. The power of the Appropriations Committee was sufficient to offset the actions of a majority of Congress *and* the president.[22]

---

[22] I should note here that the statement issued by Carter in signing the legislation was devoid of enthusiasm; the president's words did little to fuel the spending ardor of the Appropriations Committee.

RELATING TO THE DISTRICT

Obviously the central arena of most of my years in Congress was the Committee on Education and Labor, as a member of several subcommittees and as chairman of one, and my interest in education and related issues was deep. Yet I had long since realized that there was little electoral benefit back home in Indiana for all my work for education. Jack Schuster, of the Claremont Graduate School, in an essay, "An 'Education Congressman' Fights for Survival,"[23] describes my efforts in my reelection campaign of 1968 to generate, on the basis of my advocacy of education, support from schoolteachers and college professors. In terms neither of funds contributed to the campaign nor of volunteer work was the attempt very productive.

Twelve years later, when I lost my race for reelection to a twelfth term in the House, the situation had not, from my viewpoint at least, much improved. Although during twenty-two years in the House I had been chief sponsor or cosponsor of nearly every education bill enacted into law, and although if returned to Congress I not only would have remained majority whip but would have become second in seniority to Chairman Perkins on the Education and Labor Committee as well as Chairman of the House Administration Committee, with jurisdiction over campaign finance laws, neither the National Education Association, the principal teachers' association in my district, nor the American Federation of Teachers gave significant support to my campaign.

I describe this history only because so many observers of Congress are quick to charge its members with championing legislation chiefly to ingratiate themselves with a "special interest" or in Pavlovian response to constituent demands. The fact is that I could never afford, politically speaking, to as-

[23] In Allan P. Sindler, ed., *Policy and Politics in America* (Boston: Little, Brown, 1973).

sume that the measures I championed—aid to the handicapped, to children and the elderly, and to college students and support for the arts, museums, and libraries—would be appreciated on their merits alone by the voters in my home district. Ultimately it was only by "taking care of business" in my district—by tending to constituent requests, obtaining a fair share of federal dollars for local projects, and making frequent appearances at district functions—that I was able to gain the latitude I needed to be a policymaker in the national arena.

CHAPTER 4

THE LEGISLATIVE PROCESS
RECONSIDERED

WHAT ARE SOME OF THE GENERAL LESSONS I derived from my experience as a member of Congress writing education legislation? Let me single out three; all of them run against the grain of conventional wisdom.

"PASSIVE-AGGRESSIVE" CONGRESS

First, despite the assertion of many political scientists that the president is the major source of policy innovation in the system, Congress can be dominant. In 1970 Majority Leader Carl Albert, after reviewing the record of Congress on education legislation, declared, "In all these areas, the initiative for these measures came from within the Education and Labor Committee rather than from the executive branch of the government." Mr. Albert's assessment was accurate.

Certainly during the years of the Nixon and Ford administrations the executive branch had little influence on the making of federal education policy. With few exceptions education commissioners, cabinet secretaries, and presidents made no major contributions. I note some highlights of those years:

The Basic Educational Opportunity Grant for college students was first proposed by Senator Claiborne Pell. In the House, Albert Quie, Frank Thompson, and I supported Pell's effort, and in the Senate he responded to our leadership on the issue of institutional aid.

Although we were frustrated by a Nixon veto, it was Senator Mondale and I who won passage by Congress of the first major child day-care bill.

The 1974 revision of the Title I ESEA formula was the result of much negotiation and compromise, but the negotiations and the compromising took place on Capitol Hill, not between Congress and the executive.

In the Ninety-fourth Congress, Quie and I in the House and Harrison Williams of New Jersey in the Senate wrote the Education for All Handicapped Children Act.

President Nixon proposed the National Institute for Education, but my House subcommittee colleagues and I were the ones who actually designed its structure and shaped its substance.

Although our political system is so complex and fragmented that it is often difficult to understand the impact of Congress on the making of policy, the years of President Nixon produced such ongoing conflict as greatly to illumine the congressional role and heighten its visibility. These were, after all, years in which Nixon attempted to turn back the advances in education of Lyndon Johnson's Great Society. Congress resisted, successfully, and defended the Johnson programs.[1]

What is also important to understand as one examines the resurgent role of Congress during the Nixon and Ford period is that in response to the confrontationalist posture of both presidents Congress took several steps, both offensive and defensive, to strengthen its capabilities. Increased staff, the congressional budget process, the War Powers Resolution, the

[1] In the last few years we have seen a similar phenomenon as a coalition of Republicans and Democrats in Congress has resoundingly rejected President Reagan's attempts to weaken or dismantle major components of federal education programs.

legislative veto, limits on presidential impounding of funds already appropriated by Congress, more aggressive oversight—these were the weapons with which, in the conflict between president and Congress, Capitol Hill armed itself both to make its own contributions to policy and to resist what were perceived as unwarranted encroachments by the executive. In addition, under Nixon at least, the president's public support was so badly eroded that he could not maintain effective leadership of his own party.

In retrospect then, in designing and passing education measures, what was required for effective legislative leadership? I think it clear that the following conditions, all present in varying degrees over the period 1968 to 1980, significantly improved the chances of congressional initiative and influence:

1. A reluctance by the executive, stemming from either substantive or partisan considerations or both, to acknowledge problems and develop legislative proposals.

2. A variety of reforms within Congress—stronger staff and support offices for research and analysis,[2] enhanced power for the legislative leaders, greater subcommittee autonomy—all activities that allowed more time and resources for both legislating and overseeing the bureaucracy.

3. Frayed political connections between the president and his party's members in Congress to the point where they perceived little relation between their own electoral fortunes and the president's.

4. Changing career patterns and attitudes reflected in more and more younger persons serving in Congress, a decline in the power of seniority, an opening up of leadership positions to junior members, and greater interchange of personnel between Congress and the bureaucracy.

[2] Examples include the Congressional Budget Office (established in 1974) and the Office of Technology Assessment (created in 1972, began operating in 1974).

All these are among the factors that tended to make Congress, over the decade of the 1970s, less insulated from national trends, less parochial in its policy attitudes, and more aggressive in pressing its positions vis-à-vis those of the executive.

I do not suggest that every education bill was the result of intense rivalry between the two branches. In many instances the president and Congress worked together on new programs: the Higher Education Facilities Act of 1963, proposed by Kennedy and signed by Johnson; the Elementary and Secondary Education Act of 1965; the International Educational Education Act of 1966; the Arts and Humanities Endowments; and, to a lesser degree, the National Institute of Education.

My point here is straightforward: contrary to much thinking, Congress can play—has played—a powerful and creative role in the shaping of domestic legislation and in the field of education, in particular, has been a source of innovation and a forum for oversight.

My own experience, therefore, leads me to agree with political scientist Norman Ornstein's characterization of congressional power: ". . . in the lingo of psychologists, Congress today is passive-aggressive. It reacts strongly and widely to every presidential move, and it initiates action often enough to keep the executive off balance and on guard."[3] That style, of course, is in large measure what, in constructing a system of checks and balances, the framers of our Constitution intended.

"IT ALL DEPENDS"

In my analysis I have painted a picture of decision making in the American government that, I hope, demonstrates the danger of generalizing about institutional forces and individual roles. Indeed, the safest response to those who ask how pol-

[3]Norman J. Ornstein, "The New House and the New Senate," in Thomas E. Mann and Norman J. Ornstein, eds., *The New Congress* (Washington, D.C.: American Enterprise Institute, 1981), p. 381.

icy is made in the American national government is, "It all depends."

One of the most perceptive students of Congress, Gary Orfield, makes my point in these words: "Any serious attempt to describe the policy impact of Congress must obviously describe the time period, the policy areas under consideration, and the existing division of power within Congress during that period."[4] During my years in the House, I served with six presidents, three Republicans—Eisenhower, Nixon, and Ford—and three Democrats—Kennedy, Johnson, and Carter. At no point during this period was either the House or the Senate controlled by the Republicans. Yet the political environment varied enormously over those two decades and two years. The Lyndon Johnson of 1965 was not the Lyndon Johnson of 1968; the Richard Nixon of 1969 was not the Richard Nixon of 1974.[5] Both men still held the highest office in the land, but their political standing in the country and, therefore, in Congress had immensely declined in the intervening years.

So, too, although Democrats may have had a majority of seats in all eleven of the Congresses in which I served, the size of the Democratic margins in each enormously affected the calculus of political forces. Kennedy and Johnson were, of course, Democrats, and during the administrations of both, Democrats controlled both Houses of Congress. That the Democratic majorities during the Eighty-ninth Congress with Johnson were far larger and more liberal than those in the Eighty-seventh and Eighty-eighth Congresses with Kennedy goes far to explain Johnson's more productive legacy of education legislation.

During the Kennedy years the Republican-Dixiecrat coalition exercised great weight in the House of Representatives, and a Democratic president could at no point be sure that

[4]Orfield, *Congressional Power*, p. 280.
[5]And it now appears that the Ronald Reagan of 1984 will not be the Ronald Reagan of 1987.

the House would support him on education—or on anything else. When the Johnson landslide over Goldwater in 1964 brought a greater than two-to-one advantage to the Democrats in the House of Representatives (295 Democrats, 140 Republicans), the President could count on likeminded legislators to work closely with him to achieve objectives that all held in common. During the Nixon-Ford era, Nixon's almost unrelieved antagonism to the Democrats who were in the majority on Capitol Hill meant near-constant warfare between the two branches of government.

The personal style of presidents, their level of popularity, and their degree of party control of Congress influence the course of legislation. But other forces are at work as well. The increasing role of money and media in elections, the changing styles of legislators, and the internal shifts of influence in Congress, particularly in the authority of committee and subcommittee chairmen—all these factors exert significant impact on the policy process.

There were, for example, three chairmen of the House Education and Labor Committee during my time: Graham Barden of North Carolina, a crusty, ultraconservative member of the Dixiecrat establishment; Adam Clayton Powell, Jr., black, liberal, flamboyant, the voice of Harlem and a national figure; and Carl Perkins, whom I have earlier described. All three were Democrats, but in the way they saw and exercised their responsibilities, they differed radically.

The contrasting temperaments and styles of Powell and Perkins were particularly striking. Powell was a highly intelligent, charistmatic figure who took great pride in his position as chairman of the Education and Labor Committee and was not reticent about enjoying the trappings of power. He was also easily bored; he found tedious committee hearings that were not on topics of political interest to him, and he was not likely to pore over the fine print of bills. One positive result of this combination of traits was that, as chairman, Powell was glad to delegate work and responsibilities to committee mem-

bers and thereby give junior congressmen like me opportunities to develop issues and expertise on our own. Of course, I
comment here on Powell as legislative leader and not on the
troubles that ultimately led to his political and legal demise.

Carl Perkins, on the other hand, was the congressional version of a grind; he did his homework. He could sit through
hours, days, weeks, and months of hearings on a single piece
of legislation. He gave personal attention to the selection of
witnesses to appear before the committee, and he engaged in
countless conversations with other members of the House to
win support for his committee's bills. When Perkins finally
brought a measure to the floor of the House, his hard work
and careful preparation were rewarded; he usually prevailed.

In recent years the reforms in the House that have greatly
increased the powers of subcommittee chairmen have also
affected the course of education policy. Although Edith Green
and I were both northern Democrats and were both advocates
of federal aid to education, and although both of us chaired
subcommittees that handled education, those facts exhausted
the similarities between us. Our personal values and attitudes, our ages, our education, and our experience were so
different that all these factors affected the writing of national
policy for education.

I often reflected, while I was in Washington, that one way to
simulate the complexity I am describing would be to erect a
vast white wall to symbolize the House of Representatives.
The wall would be divided in two, half for each party. In the
wall would be 435 pins, one for each member, and to each pin
would be affixed threads of differing colors, the threads running from one member to another, each color representing a
different kind of relationship, such as geographic area, legislative interest, committee or subcommittee membership, sex,
race, religion, marital status, national or ethnic background,
political ideology, college or university, fraternity or sorority
or club, hobby or other extracurricular interest, and profession or career. Do the members play paddleball in the House

gymnasium? Attend the weekly prayer group? Travel abroad on the same trips? In the decentralized system that is American politics, each of these many relationships can at one point or another exert an impact on legislative outcomes.

It must also be evident that there is considerable scope in Congress for entrepreneurial legislators, members of both the House and the Senate whose principal motivation for service is the opportunity to participate in the shaping of national policy. Certainly that was my chief purpose, as I know it was for many others.

For one who has served even a few years in the United States Congress, the thought of membership in a body like the British House of Commons is most unattractive. The reason is simple. The possibility that an individual member of Parliament can initiate or create policy is—unless, of course, one is a member of the cabinet, or "government"—severely limited. That in the United States we speak of the executive branch as the "administration" rather than the "government" makes my point. Here not only the president but also Congress—and at times the courts—constitute the "government" and make national policy.

My second generalization, then, is to advise against generalizations. Identifying and isolating variables and accurately tracing cause and effect relationships are not, in the study of Congress, simple and straightforward activities.

"KNOWING WHAT IS RIGHT"

My third, and last, observation runs to the dilemma of the policymaker in search of timely and accurate information and reasoned analysis. President Johnson used to say, "My problem is not so much doing what is right but knowing what is right." Johnson's aphorism aptly characterized much of my experience as a legislator seeking to fashion sensible policies for the diversity of problems with which my colleagues and I were concerned. The truth was that on many issues we were far freer to come to our own judgments than we sometimes pretended, if only we could have obtained the facts more swiftly and in more usable form. After all, my constituents back home in Indiana did not, thank heaven, begin every day by saying to one another over the breakfast table, "I wonder what kind of formula for institutional aid Brademas is going to support in the higher education bill."

Yet the low public visibility of many of the legislative problems with which we dealt did not make them any less intractable. I concluded long ago, therefore, that crucial to the ability of legislators to do their job effectively is far better access to the best available intelligence. Woodrow Wilson, speaking not as president of the United States but as president of the American Political Science Association, put the point succinctly: "The man who has the time, the discrimination and the sagacity to collect and comprehend the principal facts and the man who must act upon them must draw near to one another and feel that they are in engaged in a common enterprise."[6]

From what I have said, it must be clear why I became a champion of steps to enable legislators and others to "collect and comprehend the principal facts" about education. I have earlier explained my advocacy of the National Institute of Education. I have also cited my frustration at not having been able, as we considered from 1969 to 1972 how best to channel assistance to colleges and universities, to obtain for our work thoughtful analyses from the higher-education community. I have further noted how several of us in Congress, distressed by the apparent failure of the universities to pay serious intellectual attention to the economics of higher education, turned elsewhere—as to the Carnegie Commission—for counsel.

On the basis of my description and analysis of the legislative

[6] Woodrow Wilson, "The Law and the Facts," Presidential Address, Seventh Annual Meeting of the American Political Science Association, as printed in *American Political Science Review* 5, no. 1 (February, 1911): 9.

process as I knew and took part in it, I offer three general conclusions:

First, in a political system often characterized as one in which presidential lawmaking is the norm, Congress, at least with respect to aid to education, has played a coequal and at times dominant role.

Second, the nature and extent of federal support for education have been shaped by a diversity of forces—personal, political, institutional—in constant interaction and flux. One searches in vain for theorems of legislative behavior that will hold true in all times and all places.

Third, constrained to reach decisions in an environment of uneven information, a legislator must often settle for tentative, proximate solutions to deep and unsettling problems.

From time to time there are those who, disagreeing with decisions that Congress has made—or not made—suggest that we change our unique constitutional system and move in the direction of a parliamentary form of government, in which the executive is better able to exert its will on a balky legislature.[7] I do not share this view. For whatever the deficiencies of Congress, no other institution so effectively exercises three functions essential to the political system of a large, restless, complex society. It is Congress, and only Congress, that can, at one and the same time, serve as vehicle of representation, formulator of public policy, and monitor of its implementation.

To paraphrase Voltaire, if Congress did not exist, it would be necessary to invent it.

---

[7]Lloyd N. Cutler, former presidential adviser to Jimmy Carter, is among the proponents of this view. He presented his case for reorganizing the American system more along parliamentary lines in a provocative article entitled "To Form a Government" that appeared in the fall, 1980, issue of *Foreign Affairs*.

PART TWO

THE NATIONAL DEBATE
ON EDUCATION:
THE FERMENT OF THE 1980s

CHAPTER 5

EDUCATION IN THE SPOTLIGHT:
A CALL FOR REFORM

TWENTY YEARS AGO, on April 11, 1965, President Lyndon Johnson sat outside the one-room schoolhouse in Stonewall, Texas, that he had attended as a child and signed into law the Elementary and Secondary Education Act, the first major program of federal aid to schools. Declared President Johnson, "I believe that no law I have signed or will ever sign means more to the future of America."

Two decades after that dramatic event education has returned to center stage. In the last few years we have seen, metaphorically speaking, a tidal wave of reports—from commissions, task forces, conferences, study groups, and individual scholars—on the need to reform American education, from the primary grades through graduate school.

This resurgence of interest should surprise no one. As we have seen in earlier chapters, social or economic stress in the United States has often been accompanied by renewed concern for education. The Morrill Act setting up the land-grant colleges in the 1860s, the GI Bill after World War II, the National Defense Education Act after the Soviet Union launched Sputnik in 1957—these educational initiatives sprang from a sense of urgency about America's capacity to adapt to changing times.

The 1980s are characterized by vast and fast-moving technological advances, but in the context of a decade and a half of economic difficulties. Since 1970 the United States has suffered three major recessions, each more severe than the one before. More Americans were out of work during the recession of 1981–82 than at any time since the Great Depression, and unemployment has since remained at historically high levels. Deficits in the federal budget from fiscal 1982 to 1986 shot up by a staggering $304 billion and threaten to reach $200 billion a year for the foreseeable future; the balance of international trade has been shifting against us; and we are in danger of losing the productivity race to Japan and West Germany.

Today the nation again looks to the educational system as a key to coping with new challenges. Can American industry and workers compete effectively in world markets? As we shift increasingly to high technology and service industries, can we produce the people with the skills these activities require? In an age of specialization are we preparing persons with the perspective to look beyond the recommendations of the experts and technicians and make the judgments required of citizens in a free, self-governing nation? In a country more and more apprehensive about the future, it is not surprising to find attention more and more focused on the institutions that, through our young people, help shape it: schools, colleges, and universities.

Nor is it unusual to discover concern about education spilling beyond classrooms into living rooms, boardrooms, and legislative committee rooms. For, in speaking of education, we speak of values—what we as a society believe important and worthy of expenditure of resources. And when we talk of resources—how to generate and allocate them—we enter the realm of politics. Values, resources, politics—all these considerations are inextricably bound up in any discussion of education.

In commenting on the recent reports and studies and the rising place of education on the national agenda, I shall argue that the success of reform depends not solely but nonetheless significantly on leadership by the federal government. I shall assert as well that Ronald Reagan has marked a sea change in the attitude of a modern American president toward the federal role in education. For despite all his rhetoric about the importance of education to our national life, President Reagan has pursued and continues to pursue policies that undermine the schools, colleges, and universities of the United States.

A CORNUCOPIA OF REPORTS: ELEMENTARY AND SECONDARY EDUCATION

The report of the National Commission on Excellence in Education, issued in April, 1983—eighteen years to the month after the signing of the Elementary and Secondary Education Act—was the first and most widely publicized statement about the condition of American education. The Commission on Excellence warned, in now familiar language, that "our schools are sinking in a rising tide of mediocrity."

The commission's report, *A Nation at Risk,* was soon followed by statements from the Education Commission of the States, the Business-Higher Education Forum, the Twentieth Century Fund, the National Science Board, and three of the nation's most respected educators, John I. Goodlad, Theodore R. Sizer, and Ernest L. Boyer.[1] Each of the reports was spon-

---

[1] The reports and studies referred to here include *A Nation at Risk: The Imperative for Education Reform,* by the National Commission on Excellence in Education (Washington, D.C., April, 1983); *Action for Excellence,* by the Task Force on Education for Economic Growth of the Education Commission of the States (Denver, Colo., June, 1983); *America's Competitive Challenge: The Need for a National Response,* by the Business-Higher Education Forum (Washington, D.C., April, 1983); *Making the Grade,* by the Twentieth Century Fund Task Force on Federal Elementary and Secondary Education Policy (New York, May, 1983); *Educating Americans for the 21st Century,* by the National Science Board Commission on Precollege Education in Mathematics, Science, and Technology (Washington, D.C., September, 1983); John I. Goodlad, *A Place Called School* (New York: McGraw-Hill, 1983); Theodore R. Sizer, *Horace's Compromise: The Dilemma of the American High School* (Boston: Houghton Mifflin, 1984); and Ernest L. Boyer, *High School: A Report on Secondary Education in America* (New York: Harper and Row, 1983). Another report, sponsored by the Committee for Economic Development, entitled *Investing in Our Chil-*

sored by a different organization, employed a different methodology, and addressed a different aspect of the education enterprise. The Commission on Excellence, chaired by David P. Gardner, now president of the University of California, was appointed by then Secretary of Education Terrel Bell and dealt chiefly with secondary schools, as did a study, *High Schools*, by Ernest L. Boyer, president of the Carnegie Foundation for the Advancement of Teaching. The Task Force on Education for Economic Growth, composed of governors as well as business, labor, and academic leaders, also concentrated on high schools and stressed preparing students for the demands of the new marketplace, while the Business–Higher Education Forum emphasized the importance of education in strengthening America's position in the world economy. The Twentieth Century Fund Task Force focused on schools in urban areas, while a Commission of the National Science Board produced what it called a "plan of action for improving mathematics, science and technology education for all American elementary and secondary students so that their achievement is the best in the world by 1995." Some of the reports focused on preparation for college; others, training for a high-technology era; others, retraining adults dislocated by economic upheavals. Recommendations included a return to academic basics; an upgrading of the status of teachers and professors; and increased involvement by parents, business leaders, and public officials in improving schools.

Despite their diversity all the reports were characterized by four common themes:

---

dren: Business and the Public Schools, was issued in September, 1985. The CED group proposed measures to improve students' skills and attitudes toward learning and working. In May, 1986, the Carnegie Forum on Education and The Economy Task Force on Teaching as a Profession issued a report, *The Nation Prepared: Teachers for the 21st Century*, which called for "revolutionary" changes in the preparation and profession of teaching, including the establishment of a national board to certify and set standards for teachers.

1. There is a national crisis in education.

2. There is an intimate link between the health of our schools, colleges, and universities and our ability to enjoy economic prosperity, ensure a strong defense, maintain a high quality of life, and safeguard the values of a free society.

3. Educators must build alliances with leaders in government, business, and labor.

4. Not only is state and local aid to education essential, but there is an indispensable role for the federal government.

There was a fifth similarity: although some of the studies addressed higher education, they did so chiefly in terms of the relationship of colleges and universities to the public schools. Higher learning, except for teacher education, was not the subject of the first stream of reform proposals. But in 1984 that picture changed as the spotlight moved to postsecondary education.

SHIFTING THE FOCUS TO HIGHER LEARNING

I hope I may be forgiven for noting an event that took place on December 1, 1983, as indicative of the shifting focus. On that date the Subcommittee on Graduate Education, which I chaired, of the National Commission on Student Financial Assistance issued its findings and recommendations, *Signs of Trouble and Erosion: A Report on Graduate Education in America.* This twelve-member bipartisan commission was created by Congress in 1980 to study student-aid programs and make recommendations for improving them. Many of the judgments of our commission about graduate education are, in my view, also true of postsecondary education generally.[2] The commission found evidence of weakness throughout the graduate enterprise: in declining enrollments of talented stu-

[2] Much of this material is drawn from the report and from a subsequent article of mine that appeared in the March, 1984, issue of *Change*, a magazine of higher education.

dents, in deterioration of the infrastructure that supports research and training, and in shortages of trained experts in key fields. Certainly many universities are encountering increasing difficulty in maintaining first-class faculties in the sciences and engineering, while in the humanities and social sciences the nation risks losing a generation of scholarship.

Enrollments of outstanding graduate students in the arts and sciences are falling. The reasons are several: the depressed state of the academic job market, demographic changes, rapidly escalating costs, and reduced financial aid. Between 1969 and 1981, for example, the total number of stipends awarded by federal agencies fell from nearly eighty thousand to approximately forty thousand. At Harvard University only one-third of the top graduates of 1980 planned traditional graduate study, compared with over three-fourths in the 1960s. Many students who thirty years ago would have pursued advanced studies now avoid graduate preparation because they see little future in it alongside opportunities in law, medicine, business, and industry.

The loss of talented students is especially marked among minorities and women. Both groups are still seriously underrepresented at the doctoral level. Blacks, Hispanics, and Native Americans constitute 19 percent of the population but are currently awarded only 8 percent of the doctoral degrees. Minority graduate students are heavily concentrated in education, and modest gains in other fields during the early 1970s are being rapidly eroded. Although women compose half the population, they received only 32 percent of the Ph.D.s awarded in 1981, and their degrees were concentrated in education, the arts, humanities, and social sciences. Huge disparities persist in the physical and natural sciences and in engineering.

Excellence in graduate training and research is impossible without first-rate facilities, yet knowledgeable observers report that the condition of university laboratories is "pathetic" and that our university libraries are unable to keep up with the explosion of published knowledge. The costs of maintaining adequate, up-to-date research facilities, especially in the sciences, can be staggering. A recent survey of scientific equipment at fifteen institutions concluded that to meet their needs over the next three years would require nearly twice what they have spent in the last four. Although expenditures for library materials rose by 91 percent in the 1970s, enormous cost increases forced a reduction of 20 percent in acquisition of new volumes.

Corporate and government leaders also warn of serious shortages of graduate-trained experts in the sciences, engineering, and international affairs. Intense foreign competition in high-technology fields and projected defense budgets totaling $2 trillion over the next five years have contributed to greatly increased domestic demand for doctoral-level scientists and engineers. The supply in these areas is expanding, though not fast enough, but the number of graduate students specializing in the study of foreign cultures and societies is shrinking.

University officials also report two developments that threaten the high quality of American graduate faculties. In such areas as engineering and computer science, particularly computer engineering, solid-state electronics, and digital systems, faculty vacancies jeopardize our capacity to produce enough new scientists to meet national needs. In other fields the problem is reversed. The depressed employment market in the humanities and social sciences means that faculty turnover is limited. Tenured faculty, in effect, block the career progression of younger academics, many of whom now make up a class of itinerant scholars wandering from campus to campus on short-term assignments, hoping one day to find an open tenured position. The commission observed that, in consequence of these trends, we are likely to lose a generation of scholarship, particularly in the humanities and the social sciences.

The deterioration of graduate education documented by the

commission is the outcome of demographic changes, specifically the end of the postwar baby-boom student population, and of dramatic shifts in corporate needs and government priorities in a period of economic retrenchment. Although it is obviously necessary to adjust to changing conditions, sharp fluctuations as well as cutbacks in government funds for graduate studies have already damaged the capacity of our universities to serve national interests. The commission concluded that, although the graduate enterprise was the responsibility of many sectors of our society—state governments, private foundations, business, and industry—indispensable to excellence in graduate education is the support of the federal government. The commission members, therefore, set forth a ten-point agenda for federal action. We recommended that the federal government undertake the following steps:

1. *Ensure support for talented graduate students.* The number of science and engineering fellowships in various federal agencies should be substantially increased. Congress should also authorize 1,250 new fellowships and awards each year to support graduate students in the arts, humanities, and social sciences. Research assistantships, work-study funds, and loan programs for graduate students in all fields should be expanded.

2. *Increase the numbers of talented women in graduate education.* Fellowship support for women graduate students should be increased with particular attention to encouraging women to enter fields of study in which they are underrepresented. The federal government and research universities should work together to disseminate information to women about opportunities in science.

3. *Increase the numbers of talented minority students in graduate education.* Funds for all programs—undergraduate, professional, and graduate—that aid minority students should be increased. Support to improve science education in predominantly minority undergraduate institutions should be

expanded, and colleges and universities should provide more assistantships to minority students.

4. *Maintain and enhance the nation's strengths in graduate research.* Federal support for basic and applied research at colleges and universities should grow with the economy at a rate at least sufficient to keep pace with inflation. To stabilize the research endeavor, the government should, wherever possible, make multiyear commitments.

5. *Ensure that graduate laboratories, equipment, and instrumentation are of high quality.* Federal funds for improving and modernizing university equipment, instruments, and laboratories should be substantially increased. Private business and industry should be encouraged, through tax incentives, to contribute equipment, both new and used, to universities.

6. *Enhance the quality of scholarly libraries and ensure that valuable collections are maintained.* Federal grants for operating support of all college and university libraries should be increased, and federal programs to improve the collections and organization of those libraries should be expanded.

7. *Attract and retain promising young scholars as faculty members.* Substantial support, in the form of multiyear salary stipends, should be provided to universities for promising young faculty members in the physical and natural sciences, engineering, the arts, humanities, and the social sciences.

8. *Meet pressing national needs for highly trained experts.* Federal support for research, instruction, and graduate study in foreign languages and cultures should be significantly increased, as should funds enabling faculty and teachers to study abroad.

9. *Evaluate the impact of the federal government's decisions on the nation's needs for men and women educated at the graduate level.* The federal government should establish a process for regular and systematic assessment of the impact of federal policies and programs on the nation's need for men and women educated at the graduate level. "Educational impact statements" would anticipate the consequences for graduate education of federal

decisions, especially budgetary ones, and better enable universities, business, and industry to respond effectively.

10. *Improve both the quantity and the quality of information about graduate education.* Appropriate departments and agencies of the federal government should work with state governments, colleges, universities, and other organizations to collect the data needed to describe and monitor the overall conditions of graduate education.

SPOTLIGHT ON COLLEGES AND UNIVERSITIES

As I have said, the signs of trouble that our commission detected in graduate research and training characterize some aspects of undergraduate teaching and learning as well. But, to reiterate, it is only recently that national attention has been turned to colleges and universities. The first of the recent studies of postsecondary education, *Involvement in Learning,* appeared in October, 1984. Sponsored by the National Institute of Education and written by seven education researchers, the report concluded, "The realities of student learning, curricular coherence, the quality of facilities, faculty morale and academic standards no longer measure up to our expectations." The NIE commission called for higher faculty pay and more emphasis on teaching, at least two years of liberal education for all undergraduates, stricter graduation requirements, proficiency tests to determine what students have learned, and research to improve learning.

A month later, in November, 1984, William J. Bennett, chairman of the National Endowment for the Humanities from 1981 to 1985 and now secretary of education, issued a report prepared by a group he appointed who assailed the state of the humanities on American campuses. This document, *To Reclaim a Legacy,* cites a sharp decline in the number of students majoring in the humanities and contends that the humanities, and particularly the study of Western civilization, have lost their central place in undergraduate education. The Bennett report recommended that colleges and universities reshape the undergraduate curriculum, basing it on "a clear vision of what constitutes an educated person," and urged agreement on a core of common studies for all students.

In December, 1984, the Association of American Colleges published a survey sharply criticizing the baccalaureate degree. The AAC committee said that undergraduate degree programs had been devalued with the curriculum often fragmented and overspecialized. The study exhorted faculties to rise above narrow departmental concerns and take responsibility for the entire curriculum.

The AAC committee proposed requiring study in nine areas that emphasize intellectual capacities rather than factual knowledge. The areas are: inquiry and critical analysis, literacy, understanding numerical data, historical consciousness, science, values, art, international and multicultural experiences, and methods of in-depth research and learning.

More recently Howard R. Bowen and Jack H. Schuster published the findings of their survey of the American professoriat, *American Professors: A National Resource Imperiled.* The authors estimate that to meet future teaching and research needs American colleges and universities must recruit nearly half a million persons for professorial ranks over the next twenty-five years. Yet Bowen and Schuster report that there has been a gravitational shift of students—among them the most academically gifted—*away* from careers in the academy.

Certain needs were identified in all these studies of postsecondary education:[3] the need for a more rigorous curriculum, for a reaffirmation of the liberal arts, and for assumption by administrators and faculty of more responsibility for meeting the problems of undergraduate education. The reports also agreed on the importance of higher faculty pay and greater faculty commitment to teaching.[3]

[3] A new study from the Carnegie Foundation for the Advancement of Teaching, released in September, 1985, also concentrated on postsecondary education. The report, *Higher Education and the American Resurgence*, was written by Frank Newman, president of the Education Commission of the States.

Here I think it important to make two observations. First, at least in my view, the problems of our colleges and universities are not as grim as those of our grade and high schools and are far less severe than some critics contend. Commenting on the NIE study, Terrel Bell said, "American higher education has the sniffles, [but] no one should conclude that we are poorly served" by our colleges and universities.[4]

The reports, moreover, contain analytical flaws. The NIE panel, for example, cites falling scores on the Graduate Record Examination as one sign of a decline in the quality of higher education. But GRE scores are not representative of American college students. Students who do not plan to go to graduate school or who apply for law or business school do not take these examinations. As an aside, I note that the Graduate Management Aptitude Test scores for students applying to business school went up ten points in the last two years, while from 1970 to 1982 Law School Aptitude Test scores also rose.

Second, colleges and universities are already correcting many of the deficiencies described in the reports. For example, Harvard, the University of Pennsylvania, Emory University, Middlebury College, and Brooklyn College have restored to the undergraduate curriculum a broad-based general-education component, either through establishing distribution requirements or by introducing core courses.

New York University requires that undergraduates in professionally oriented programs take courses in the liberal arts and sciences. In addition, beginning in the fall of 1981, NYU

Newman calls for reforms to help colleges and universities produce the scholars and research needed to keep America economically competitive and prepare graduates for a life of involved citizenship. Refocused and increased federal student aid, coupled with more attention to applied research, can help meet both these objectives, concludes Newman.

[4] As quoted in *Higher Education and National Affairs* 33, no. 21 (November 5, 1984): 1.

instituted a new core curriculum for students in the College of Arts and Science. This program stresses interdisciplinary learning and includes rigorous courses in writing and mathematics, philosophy and religion, the natural sciences, and Western and non-Western civilizations. In addition, all freshmen in the College of Arts and Science at New York University must take a full year of expository writing and pass a proficiency test in writing.

Another recent heartening development is a Modern Language Association study indicating that, in a reversal of a twelve-year trend, enrollments in foreign-language courses at American colleges and universities are now on the upswing. A survey by the American Council on Education also found that two-thirds of our colleges and universities require entering students to take placement tests in English and mathematics and that 90 percent of the institutions are making curricular or other changes to improve the quality of their undergraduate programs. Much remains to be done but progress is under way.

Taken together, all the reports and their recommendations cited in this chapter chart a path for substantial improvement of education at every level. But will the reformers achieve their agendas? In evaluating the prospects, I see one overwhelming obstacle: inadequate resources. The capacity of the schools, colleges, and universities of the United States to achieve excellence depends on sufficient support from state and local governments, private individuals, families and students, foundations, business and industry—and the federal government.

THE ROLE OF THE FEDERAL GOVERNMENT IN EDUCATION

Let me put my views in context. I am a strong champion of a dominant role for state and local governments in elementary and secondary education and believe that the states are vital to higher education as well. During the past few years, in fact, many states have made innovative and in some instances politically courageous efforts to upgrade schools, improve teacher training, and strengthen curricula.[5]

The American system of education—and, indeed, of government—is more decentralized than that of most other Western democracies. This decentralization allows a broad measure of local influence and freedom of decision making. This is as it should be. Since the earliest days of the Republic, local control of education has been a deeply-rooted tradition. Yet even as there is a major responsibility for state and local governments in education, there is an essential place for the national government as well. My experience of nearly a quarter century in public life has convinced me that there are certain spheres of activity in which involvement of the federal government in education is not only appropriate but indispensable. These spheres are:

1. To ensure effective access to an opportunity for education.

2. To support research on how people teach and learn.

3. To target help to populations in special need, such as the handicapped and the disadvantaged.

4. To act as a catalyst for state and local educational efforts.

5. To provide support for initiatives in areas of critical national need.

Let me, drawing on my own background as a national legislator, touch briefly on each of these federal purposes. Several measures that Congress, with support from both Republicans and Democrats, has passed in the last two decades were a direct expression of our concern that an opportunity for a college education should not be denied any talented and motivated student because of financial need. Toward that end Congress constructed a fabric of student-aid programs, including Guaranteed Student Loans, College Work-Study, and

---

[5] *The Nation Responds,* a document issued by the Department of Education in May, 1984, catalogs an array of state and local efforts to enhance education.

Pell Grants. Since their inception these programs have provided millions of American young people the opportunity to go to college. The ideology was simple and straightforward: desire and ability, not wealth, should be the key to educational opportunity.

A second area of unique responsibility for the national government is educational research. Why? One reason is that state and local governments are not likely to have the financial resources necessary to support sophisticated analysis of the fundamental processes of learning and teaching.

As I have said earlier, I became a vigorous champion of the National Institute of Education, the principal federal agency supporting research in education, when it was proposed by someone with whom I disagreed on many matters, President Nixon. When Nixon suggested the Institute in his Education Message to Congress in 1970, I thought it a splendid initiative and immediately communicated my enthusiasm to the appropriate officials at the Department of Health, Education, and Welfare. "I want the bill in my subcommittee. I'll handle it, push it, pass it," I said.

Educational research, I can attest, in commanding the attention of elected politicians, is not the most riveting of subjects. Politicians are by nature impatient and want immediate results; they have little interest in tracing the often tortuous connections between initial research efforts and final educational outcomes. Those of us who advocated increased attention to research made the point that we earmarked for "R&D"—research and development—a substantial percentage of the annual federal budgets for defense, agriculture, and health. Yet when it came to education, with its enormous impact on our society, the nation was not spending the small amount needed to develop thoughtful, objective, scientific evidence on what was effective in education and what was not. Eventually my colleagues on the Select Education Subcommittee, which I chaired, of the House Education and Labor Committee acted, and in 1972 Congress passed the legislation that created the NIE.[6] A third appropriate federal activity is to ensure at least a degree of attention to groups of learners who would otherwise be ignored. A prime example is socioeconomically disadvantaged children. In Congress, I was a member of the subcommittee that wrote the Elementary and Secondary Education Act (ESEA) of 1965, one of Lyndon Johnson's weapons in the War on Poverty. That legislation, among other purposes, provides federal funds to school districts with large numbers of low-income children.

Why did we write this bill? When I arrived in Congress in 1959, state governments were not much interested in poor children, especially those living in cities or in remote rural areas. For example, in my native Indiana state government policies were strongly influenced by such groups as the chamber of commerce and the farm bureau, which had little interest in the well-being of people living in urban areas. Many of us in Congress and some presidents of both parties perceived that there were indeed genuine needs—in housing, health, and education—to which state and city governments were

[6] Under the tenure of Secretary Bennett the National Institute of Education has been caught up in a general reorganization of the research activities of the Department of Education. Specifically, Bennett has moved to abolish NIE as an autonomous entity and place all research functions under the assistant secretary for educational research and improvement. On this matter I agree with former Secretary Terrel Bell, who has said that he would have preferred the reverse solution: abolish the assistant secretary's post and put all research under the NIE. Another education program I helped bring about, the Fund for the Improvement of Postsecondary Education, has also been the subject of recent controversy. Envisioned as a venture capital fund for innovative and promising projects to enhance teaching and learning on the nation's campuses, FIPSE has from the beginning relied on the judgment of independent and respected educators and researchers in the field to decide on priorities and assess worthy proposals. Working against this tradition of independence, Secretary Bennett has attempted to intervene in the process and to set as FIPSE's research priorities the issues in which he is interested. The secretary's efforts met with broad, immediate, and bipartisan opposition, not only from the chairman of the FIPSE Board (himself a Republican) but also from important members of Congress of both parties, including the members of the House and Senate appropriations committees responsible for funding FIPSE.

simply not responding. It was this inattention by state and local political leaders, therefore, that prompted us at the federal level to say, "We're going to do something about such problems." And we did.

Another activity warranting federal attention is the education of handicapped children. When my colleagues and I on the Select Education Subcommittee began looking into this question, we learned that millions of handicapped children of school age were receiving either inadequate education or none at all. We therefore wrote PL 94-142, the Education of All Handicapped Children Act. That legislation has distressed some state and local officials because it requires them to provide a free, appropriate education for all handicapped children. In fact, when Congress initiated the law, more than forty states already had their own mandates for educating handicapped children, by state constitution, statute, or court order. The states were simply refusing to enforce the provisions of their own laws.

The history of the Education for All Handicapped Children Act was not a case of a few congressmen suddenly deciding that the federal government would impose some onerous mandate on state and local governments to do something they did not want to do. Rather, my principal House cosponsor, Republican Albert M. Quie, and I wrote a statute that gave states and local school systems additional resources to do what by their own laws they should have been doing but were failing to do.

The history of PL 94-142 also demonstrates the fourth responsibility of the federal government, to spur state and local educational activities. It should be emphasized in this regard that today federal support of public elementary and secondary education is, as a proportion of total expenditures, on the order of 6.4 percent. At issue then is neither an enormous percentage of money nor an aggrandizement by the national government of responsibility for making decisions for the schools. Nor do I advocate that state and local control of elementary and secondary schools should be in any way diminished. The role of the federal government in education should, for the most part, focus on the margins where a modest investment can yield significant dividends.

Finally, there is a place for federal activity in areas of critical national need. An early example can be found in President Eisenhower's advocacy of the 1958 National Defense Education Act, which provided federal funds to improve the teaching of science, mathematics, and modern foreign languages. Similarly, in recent months there has been a surge of interest in producing more teachers of science and mathematics, fields in which the United States is experiencing a desperate shortage. With strong support from both Republicans and Democrats, Congress in 1984 passed legislation authorizing $425 million a year to increase the supply of science and mathematics teachers in elementary and high schools and to provide sabbaticals for such teachers to take refresher courses.[7]

Having outlined the areas in education where federal assistance over the last quarter-century has brought positive results, I return to the current debate on education reform. One need only scan the reports and studies I have earlier discussed to recognize that every one of them makes clear that, in financing American education, there are significant responsibilities for business, foundations, and individuals as well as all levels of government. The Twentieth Century Fund Task Force, for example, in *Making the Grade,* calls for more federal funds for elementary and secondary schools. The task force observes:

> The federal government, after all, is charged with providing for the security and well-being of our democratic society, which rest largely on a strong and competent system of public education. . . .

---

[7] In fiscal 1985, Congress appropriated $100 million for this program; in fiscal 1986, $45 million (subsequently reduced to $43 million under the first round of Gramm-Rudman cuts).

... educating the young is a compelling national interest, and ... action by the federal government can be as appropriate as action by state and local governments.

In *Action for Excellence* the Education Commission of the States concludes:

> For decades, the Federal Government has played a role in giving special educational help to groups in special need; in helping guarantee access for the disadvantaged to education; in supporting student aid, research and development, and in helping meet the nation's critical labor needs. This is no time for the Federal Government to shirk these responsibilities or to shrink suddenly from the issue of education as a national priority. The Federal Government's role, to be sure, is a supporting role. But the role is essential.

In his study on high schools Ernest Boyer also insists that "to achieve excellence in education, the Federal Government . . . must be a partner in the process."

And what of the recommendations of the National Commission on Excellence in Education, commissioned by the Reagan administration? The report is unequivocal:

> The Federal Government, in cooperation with states and localities, should help meet the needs of key groups of students such as the gifted and talented, the socioeconomically disadvantaged, minority and language minority students, and the handicapped.
>
> In addition, we believe the Federal Government's role includes several functions of national consequence that states and localities alone are unlikely to be able to meet: protecting constitutional and civil rights for students and school personnel; collecting data, statistics, and information about education generally; supporting curriculum improvement and research on teaching, learning, and the management of schools; supporting teacher training in areas of critical shortage or key national needs; and providing student financial assistance and research and graduate training.
>
> The Federal Government has the *primary responsibility* [italics in original] to identify the national interest in education.

In light of this language it is not surprising that members of the National Commission on Excellence were said to have been "flabbergasted" when President Reagan responded to their report by saying that he was pleased that the commission had opposed "an end to federal intrusion" in the nation's school system. The president then added, "So, we'll continue to work in the months ahead for passage of tuition tax credits, vouchers, educational savings accounts, voluntary school prayer, and abolishing the Department of Education."

The President's interpretation was strikingly at odds with the actual content of the report. Not only did the commission explicitly endorse federal education programs that the Reagan administration has been opposing, but the commissioners totally ignored the major policies the administration has been advocating. At no point in its report did the commission say a word about prayer in public schools, tax credits to families with children in private schools, educational vouchers, or elimination of the Department of Education.

The chairman of the Excellence Commission, David P. Gardner, president of the University of California, recently reasserted the commissioners' conclusion that there is a "critical place" for the federal government in education. Speaking at a national conference to celebrate the third anniversary of *A Nation at Risk*, Gardner declared:

> Now that . . . it is clear that educational reform is a high priority nationally, this is the time for the Federal government to consider programmatic initiatives that will complement and reinforce the educational reform movement as it has taken shape at the state and local levels. . . . Federal initiatives taken now would remind the country that the Federal government remains capable of seizing opportunities and making progress that both benefit the nation and sustain the vitality of our schools, and of doing so even when confronted with conflicting and competing budgetary priorities. Congress and the President have a splendid opportunity to display leadership at this critical juncture.[8]

[8]Speech delivered at Salt Lake City, Utah, April 25, 1986.

In fashioning a program to strengthen American education, what leadership have we received from the present administration in Washington? The answer is not much. Indeed, the administration of Ronald Reagan has been more hostile to education than any other administration in the nation's history. This is a strong charge, but the Reagan record on education affords irrefutable evidence of its validity.

Mr. Reagan has repeatedly attempted to diminish if not destroy federal support of education. His budgets have called for deep slashes in aid to schools, colleges, and universities. His current secretary of education, the highest-ranking government official dealing with education, has made public statements contemptuous of the values of a college education. And the president has urged changes in our tax laws that would work great damage to public schools as well as to colleges and universities, both public and private.

It is to the Reagan record on education that I turn in the next chapter.

CHAPTER 6

EDUCATION UNDER ASSAULT:
THE COMMITMENT IMPERILED

RONALD REAGAN has never made a secret of his desire to reduce—indeed, eliminate—the role of the federal government in education. For example, over a decade ago, in a speech in Minnesota, Mr. Reagan advocated the abolition of the Office of Education in what was then the Department of Health, Education, and Welfare. Former Governor Reagan said then, without qualification, that the federal government "should not be involved in education." President Reagan's hostility toward federal support for education is not, therefore, a recent phenomenon but reflects a conviction he feels deeply and has felt for many years.

As president, Mr. Reagan's policies for education have been concise: do away with the Department of Education, encourage prayer in public schools, enact tuition tax credits and family educational allowances to help middle- and upper-income parents, offer vouchers to encourage students to attend private schools, and weaken federal regulations, including those aimed at enforcing civil rights and improving opportunities for disadvantaged and handicapped children. The Reagan administration has also pressed for massive cuts in most education budgets.

As a university president, I have been particularly distressed by the Reagan war on federal funds for higher education generally and student financial aid in particular. These programs—Guaranteed Student Loans, College Work-Study, Pell Grants—upon which millions of young Americans rely to go to college have been among the hardest hit by the Reagan budget cuts. From his first days in office the second secretary of education in the Reagan administration, William J. Bennett, has issued a series of provocative comments calling into question both the seriousness of students and the capacity of institutions of higher learning. Finally, President Reagan has urged changes in our tax laws that would work great damage not only on public schools but also on colleges and universities, both public and private, throughout the United States.

Before considering the consequences of this drive against education, I want first to identify and then to rebut the administration's central complaints against federal support for education.

REAGAN REBUTTED

Since taking office in 1981, President Reagan has consistently asserted in speeches, articles, and interviews that "the greatest public school system the world had ever seen" began to deteriorate "when the federal government started intervening." Such statements by an American president obviously raise fundamental questions about the value of using federal tax dollars to assist education.

Although he and his spokesmen rarely make their case so explicitly, Mr. Reagan's opposition to federal involvement proceeds along three lines. First, it is charged that federal influence on schools and colleges has been so massive over the last two decades that the national government has usurped roles traditionally played by state and local governments, private institutions, and families.

Is this true? By the administration's own estimates, of the $230 billion expended on *all* levels of education from *all* sources in the United States in 1983, the federal government accounted for only 9 percent. Of the total, 39 percent was provided by the states, 24 percent by local governments; and

28 percent by other sources, such as tuition and fees, endowment income, and private gifts.

Department of Education statistics also show that the federal share of receipts by public elementary and secondary schools grew from 7.9 percent in 1965–66 to 9.8 percent in 1980–81. That figure has declined to an estimated 6.4 percent in 1983–84, and 1985–86, chiefly because of budget cuts in education programs under the Reagan administration. Over the period 1965–66 to 1980–81 the portion the schools received from the states rose from 39.1 to 45.7 percent. During the 1980–82 recession, as revenues fell, many states reduced spending on education. Recently, however, most state education expenditures have begun to recover, although there exists considerable variation among regions.

A related claim is that federal assistance is not needed. Yet as I have earlier made clear, the evidence from the reports of all the task forces and commissions of the last several years, including the administration's own Commission on Excellence, flatly contradicts this contention.

A second Reagan criticism is that with federal funds for education come onerous and expensive rules and regulations that distort the proper balance of responsibility among federal, state, and local governments. Yet a study released in 1983 by the Educational Testing Service, *The Interaction of Federal and State Education Programs*, found that federal involvement in education has not, as alleged, imposed harsh burdens on the states but, on the contrary, has strengthened state education agencies.

The ETS survey, prepared for the Department of Education, described the effects in eight states of the major federal categorical programs in education. Included in the analysis were the Education for All Handicapped Children Act; the Vocational Education Act; civil rights statutes pertaining to discrimination; and provisions of the Elementary and Secondary Education Act involving compensatory programs, instructional materials, state-agency management, and bilingual education.

The findings of the ETS researchers are myth-shattering. Says their report:

> This study reveals the system of federal-state governance of education to be robust and diverse. Both the Federal government and the states appear strong actors in determining the direction of education policy. . . .
>
> Relative to 15 years ago . . . we found an improved state capacity to administer education programs—whether federal or state. This improved capacity, however, remains dependent on federal funds for the immediate future. . . .
>
> The study indicates no significant general intergovernmental conflict between the states and the Federal government.[1]

Mr. Reagan's third indictment of federal investment in education is that it has been a waste of money—that federal education programs have simply failed in their purposes. What is the evidence here? The period of federal "intervention" to which President Reagan refers began in 1958 with the National Defense Education Act enacted at the urging of President Eisenhower. The NDEA was followed by approval of an entire series of programs, supported, with varying degrees of enthusiasm, but supported nonetheless, by Presidents Kennedy, Johnson, Nixon, Ford, and Carter, as well as, for the most part, coalitions of Democrats and Republicans in Congress.

The outpouring of legislation that began in the mid-1960s and continued through the 1970s—the Elementary and Secondary Education Act, Head Start, the several higher-education acts, and the Education for All Handicapped Children Act, among others—has resulted in both substantially improving access to education and raising the levels of

---

[1] *The Interaction of Federal and Related State Education Programs* (Princeton, N.J.: Educational Testing Service, February, 1983), p. v.

achievement for many Americans who, for reasons of poverty, disability, or discrimination, had in the past been denied educational opportunity. Many examples can be cited of the effectiveness of these programs.

A RECORD OF SUCCESS

Compensatory Education

Title I (renamed Chapter 1 in 1981) of the Elementary and Secondary Education Act has channeled billions of federal dollars to states and local school districts for compensatory education. Currently representing 34 percent of all federal expenditures on elementary and secondary education, Chapter 1 is the largest program of federal support for education. Several studies have demonstrated the success of Chapter 1. In its *Annual Evaluation Report* for fiscal 1981, the Department of Education issued these findings:

> Title I services are well targeted to schools in poor areas—84 percent of the nation's elementary schools with more than half their students from poor families offer such programs—which are directed primarily to low-achieving students.
> Title I services are effective in improving performance in reading and mathematics.
> Title I students in grades in 1 to 6 in mathematics and in grades 1 to 3 in reading progressed over the course of a school year more than would be expected for them without the program. Moreover, Title I effects were found to persist over the next summer and school year, even after services ended.

Several independent studies have also shown a narrowing of the gap between black and white students' test scores on standardized tests nationally, an achievement many observers trace to Title I. The executive director of the National Assessment of Educational Progress[2] has stated that, while NAEP data cannot establish cause-and-effect correlations, the im-

[2] The National Assessment of Educational Progress is a federally financed program now run by the Educational Testing Service that regularly admin-

proved reading scores between 1970 and 1980 of nine- and thirteen-year-old black children, children from disadvantaged urban and rural schools, and nine- and thirteen-year-olds in the South can be attributed, at least in part, to Title I.[3]

President Reagan has frequently declared that increases in federal funds for education, particularly for ESEA, have been accompanied by steadily dropping test scores. Former Secretary of Education Terrel Bell always carefully avoided suggesting such a cause-and-effect relationship. Indeed, Bell told a congressional committee in 1981 that Title I programs "are successful." He concluded, "I can tell you that American education has learned how to educate disadvantaged children."[4]

But what of the declining test scores? In the spring of 1984 the Library of Congress (through its Congressional Research Service) published a study on the impact of ESEA Chapter 1 funds on learning outcomes. The study makes clear that it is simply false to suggest, as President Reagan has repeatedly done, a direct correlation between falling SAT scores and rising federal expenditures on elementary and secondary education. In fact, as the Library of Congress analysis points out, pupils who take SAT tests are not even the same children who are targets and beneficiaries of the ESEA programs. The report found the data "inconsistent with the hypothesis that federal programs have tended to decrease the achievement levels of those pupils *directly* [italics in original] affected by them."[5] The key word here is "directly." For the bulk of federal aid to elementary and secondary schools has been concentrated on disadvantaged students, many of them minority students, and those *least* likely to be taking the standardized

---

isters standardized tests to measure the educational progress of children and teenagers.
[3] As reported in "Title I Turns 20," *Education Week*, May 1, 1985, p. 12.
[4] As reported by Fred Hechinger in *New York Times*, April 23, 1985.
[5] Wayne C. Riddle, "Achievement Score Trends and Federal Involvement in Elementary and Secondary Education: An Exploration of Their Relationship," May 3, 1984.

achievement tests. An official of the College Board, which administers the SAT tests, warned in congressional testimony:

> To focus federal effort on some populations and then to measure the achievement of some other totally different population and conclude the federal effort caused the achievement of the latter to decline, is shoddy reasoning at best.[6]

Graduates of schools with disadvantaged populations that have received federal aid have in the last few years been doing better in the SAT examinations. In figures recently released by the College Board SAT scores of black high school seniors rose by seven points between 1982–83 and 1983–84. For those whom it was designed to serve, therefore, federal support is making a significant and positive difference.

Beyond these arguments, there is recent heartening news that SAT test scores of students in all states and of all races and sexes are rising. The College board reported that the 1985 class of high school seniors bound for college registered the biggest gain in average SAT scores in more than twenty years. I cite this trend only to rebut the assertion of a direct correlation between rising federal expenditures on education and declining pupil test scores. Nor do I argue that improving test scores are proof of adequate federal efforts. I remain skeptical of the great simplifiers.

Early Childhood Programs

Compensatory education measures are not the only ones launched under the banner of the Great Society that have demonstrated positive results. For example, Edward R. Zigler, an early-childhood expert at Yale University and director of the Office of Child Development in the Nixon administration, has recorded evidence of substantial gains in the achievements of children served by Head Start. In a 1979 study Zigler reported that of the one-third of Head Start children found to

[6] As reported in ibid.

suffer from illness or a physical handicap 75 percent had been treated; Head Start children repeatedly performed better on preschool achievement tests than poor children who had not participated in the program; and Head Start children scored higher on a "social competence" scale which included such variables as healthy self-image, motivation, curiosity, and independence.

Compelling data on the benefits of early educational intervention of high quality are found in a landmark research experiment conducted in Michigan. Begun in the 1960s, the project, the first phase of which was completed in 1984, followed the progress of a group of black children in Ypsilanti. The results were unequivocal: black children who sixteen years earlier at the age of three had been exposed to preschool education have grown up more successfully, academically and personally, than have a comparable group without such training.

The Ypsilanti study, *Changed Lives,* produced these findings:

1. The rates of employment and college or vocational school attendance for the preschool group at age nineteen were nearly double those of youths without the preschool program.

2. Teenage pregnancies among preschool girls were slightly more than half those among the nonpreschoolers.

3. Preschool graduates were involved in 20 percent fewer arrests and detentions.

4. 20 percent fewer preschoolers dropped out of high school.[7]

A March, 1985, report, using data drawn from New York City, confirmed the research conducted in the small-city surroundings of Ypsilanti. Martin Deutsch, Theresa Jordan, and

[7]John R. B. Clements, Lawrence J. Schwinhart, W. Steven Barnett, Ann S. Epstein, and David P. Weikart, *Changed Lives: The Effects of the Perry Preschool Program on Youths Through Age Nineteen* (Ypsilanti, Mich.: High-Scope Press, 1984).

Cynthia Deutsch, of the Institute for Developmental Studies at New York University, followed the progress of New York City inner-city children twenty years after their participation in an early forerunner of Head Start. The authors' conclusions:

> Benefits are most clearly seen in such areas of practical and social importance as job status and higher education. . . .
>
> Our findings support the notion that it is possible to make a significant difference in a youngster's life through early and sustained educational enrichment.[8]

Education of the Handicapped

Another legislative initiative, the Education for All Handicapped Children Act of 1975, was created to assist states and local school systems in providing a "free appropriate public education" to all handicapped school age children. P.L. 94-142, as the statute is known, has been called the premier educational-policy achievement for the handicapped. The legislation has been a success in several ways:

1. *Number of children served:* Since the passage of P.L. 94-142, the number of children identified as handicapped and receiving special education and related services has increased continuously. The Department of Education reported a total of 4,341,399 handicapped children in special education classes in the 1983–84 school year. In school year 1976–77 special education was serving 7.25 percent of the school-age population; by the 1982–83 school year that percentage was 9.36. If one takes into account the decline in overall school enrollments during this period, it can be postulated that P.L. 94-142 increased the number of handicapped children experiencing special education by approximately 25 percent.

2. *Teaching personnel:* Even as more and more handicapped

[8]Martin Deutsch, Theresa Jordan, and Cynthia Deutsch, "Long-Term Effect of Early Intervention: Summary of Selected Findings" (unpublished research paper, March, 1985).

pupils have begun receiving special education, the number of persons who serve them has also expanded. In 1976–77 there were 179,804 special education teachers; in 1982–83, that figure had leaped to 241,079, a growth of one-third. Similarly, over the same period, the number of support personnel such as psychologists, therapists, and aides serving handicapped children and youth rose by nearly 50 percent.

3. *Least restrictive environment:* There has also been a steady trend toward including children with more severe handicaps in the setting of regular schools as well as wider use of alternative settings and services needed for a "least restrictive" education.

Student Loans and Grants

Federal student financial-aid programs, particularly grants designed for low- and middle-income students, have been extremely important in enhancing access to higher education. Today the federal government provides over $12 billion a year in assistance to postsecondary students. Most of this aid is distributed through five federal programs—Pell Grants, Guaranteed Student Loans, College Work-Study, Supplemental Education Opportunity Grants, and National Direct Student Loans.

The largest of the grant programs, the Pell Grants, were established by the Education Amendments of 1972 for undergraduates who can show financial need. Since 1973, Pell Grants have assisted approximately 18 million students. In the 1984–85 academic year an estimated 3 million students received Pell Grants ranging from $200 to $1,900. Over half these students, 55 percent, come from families with annual incomes of $9,000 or under.

The essential components of federal student aid are as follows:

Federally insured and subsidized loans. The largest of these, Guaranteed Student Loans, provided nearly $8 billion to 3 million students in 1984–85. Since its inception in 1966, the GSL program has made loans available to more than 21 million college students.

College Work-Study. This program helps students work their way through college. In fiscal 1984, CWS provided jobs to 810,000 students.

Incentive Grants to encourage states to offer scholarships to students (SSIG). In 1972, when the program was started, only twenty-seven of the fifty-eight states and territories had their own student-aid measures; today fifty-seven have them.

Supplemental Educational Opportunity Grants (SEOG) and National Direct Student Loans (NDSL), so-called campus-based student aid. Colleges and universities receive annual allocations of federal funds for these programs, which the institutions then award to individual students who demonstrate financial need.

The primary goal of this constellation of federal student-aid measures is to overcome the financial obstacles that may dissuade or prevent students from pursuing postsecondary education. These programs have made it possible for millions of students to attend colleges, universities, and vocational institutions who twenty years ago would not have had the chance.

This survey of federal support for education is not comprehensive; I have focused on the most significant areas. The record of these programs' effectiveness is, as Secretary of Education Bell said of Title I of ESEA, "well documented." That there is room for improving their administration (and that of nearly every other federal program) there can be little doubt. But Mr. Reagan's repeated allegation that federal efforts to assist education have failed and are a waste of money simply cannot be substantiated.

Taken together, these statistics offer compelling evidence that support by the federal government has enhanced, not undermined, education in the United States. Facts and figures, of course, miss the human side of the picture, the hundreds of thousands of children and young adults whose lives have been changed for the better as a result of resources made available by our national government.

THE HUMAN DIMENSION

The statistical data do not, for example, record the pride of the Head Start teacher who has dedicated two decades to her work and witnessed the results of her labor in the most human of terms:

> It's been a great 20 years. . . . Last week a parent came up to me and said, "Aren't you Mrs. Baines? You had my little boy in Head Start. I'm going to have him come by and see you. He's in 12th grade now."
> When he came by, I looked up at this tall boy and said, "This can't be." I talked to him and asked him how he was doing in school. He is in an advanced math class and an advanced reading class. I was so proud of that boy. It just makes you feel so good, knowing you had a part in that. When you're there with those kids every day, maybe you don't see it, but once they leave you and someone tells you they're doing well, that's the rewarding part. Then you can really say, "Head Start works."[9]

The data miss the promise of vulnerable persons given a chance to achieve. In July, 1983, the *New York Times* carried a front-page article on the growing numbers of young men and women with serious physical handicaps who are entering the professions—science, medicine, and law. More and more handicapped persons, the report said, now have the academic credentials for admission to professional schools:

> The Education for All Handicapped Children Act of 1975 guaranteed handicapped children "free appropriate education" in the least restrictive environment and now handicapped chil-

---

[9] As quoted in "Head Start at 20," *Education Week,* May 8, 1985, p. 21.

dren are studying laboratory science, advanced mathematics and other courses that were sometimes closed to the disabled when they were tutored individually or enrolled in special classes.[10]

The article highlighted the accomplishments of a twenty-eight-year-old neurosurgeon at Columbia-Presbyterian Medical Center who was born with a spinal defect and wears a leg brace—one of eight hundred physically impaired physicians in the United States.

The statistical data do not reveal the drama of real-life students struggling to obtain a college education. Here are profiles of some recipients of federal aid who studied at New York University in 1984–85:

Student A is a freshman from Long Island who is living in a university dormitory. His father died in an automobile accident in 1983, leaving his mother the sole supporter of the student and his brother, also in college. Their mother has worked for seven years as a housekeeper, and student A worked in a grocery store while he was in high school. The total income of student A's family in 1983 was $4,089. The cost of attending NYU in 1984–85 was $13,158.

Student A received a scholarship from the university ($2,170) and student aid from New York State ($2,700) and had a part-time job ($2,500). These sources totaled $7,370. Clearly, to study at New York University, student A still needed federal grants and loans.

Student B has come from a southern state to New York University's Tisch School of the Arts. His father has worked for an airline for fifteen years but because of the company's financial difficulties was recently compelled to take a pay cut. Student B's mother is a writer. The parents' income in 1983 was $32,673; they can contribute no more than $3,000 a year toward their

[10] "Disabled in Professions Grow," *New York Times*, July 18, 1983.

son's education. Even with a generous NYU scholarship ($3,770) in 1984–85, student B had to rely on federal aid in the form of grants, loans, and college work-study to meet the annual cost of $13,158 in tuition, fees, room, and board.

Student C, a resident of New York City, commutes to classes at New York University. She is one of three children in a family in which both parents are employed. The family income in 1983 was $33,232. NYU calculated that her parents could contribute $3,912 toward the $10,600 she needed to pay tuition and fees in 1984–85. Student C was already receiving a $3,520 scholarship from the university and a New York State Scholarship of $1,813. Federal loans and a college work study job were essential to her ability to make up the difference. Student C's sister began college in 1985–86, increasing the family's financial burden.

None of these young people would have been able to attend New York University if Congress had approved the Reagan administration's proposed budget for college aid. Certainly none of these students fits the picture painted by Secretary Bennett of fun-loving, pampered young men and women abusing student-aid programs to finance a high-style campus life. These actual cases point to a broader reality: students today use every possible means—family support, state aid, scholarships, federal loans and grants, and work—to finance their college education.

THE REAGAN RECORD

Despite the record of progress extending from early-childhood development to services for the handicapped to improved access to a college education, the Reagan administration has mounted a steady attack against all these programs. The Reagan record on education includes proposing budget cuts for Chapter 1 ESEA programs for disadvantaged children; cuts for help in teaching handicapped children; and cuts in loans and grants to college and university students. Mr. Reagan has also called for consolidating elementary- and secondary-education programs into block grants to states and local school systems, thereby abandoning the federal responsibility to target these programs on specific needs. One example of an initiative that has suffered in this way is the Emergency School Aid Program to help schools desegregate.

Particularly damaging have been the reductions in student aid, such as Guaranteed Loans, Pell Grants, and College Work-Study. Between 1980 and 1985 total funds for student aid dropped 15 percent. The Reagan budgets for fiscal 1986 and 1987, calling for annual cuts of nearly 25 percent below previous-year levels, continue the attack.

Among the proposals offered at one point or another by the Reagan administration over the last six years have been these: to eliminate all graduate-education programs in the Department of Education; to restrict access to Pell Grants; to cap eligibility for Guaranteed Student Loans at various income levels; and to eliminate about a dozen programs designed to strengthen academic quality, such as aid for libraries, international education, and facilities renovation.

The latest Reagan higher-education budget was followed by a rash of inaccurate, even offensive, statements by Secretary of Education Bennett. Mr. Bennett, who assumed office in early 1985, accused colleges and universities of "ripping off" students and said that he would give his son $50,000 to enter business rather than Harvard. The secretary of education then insulted American college students by characterizing them as preoccupied with cars, stereos, and three-week vacations at the beach. He next charged that 13,000 students from families with incomes exceeding $100,000 were receiving federally guaranteed loans, a representation demonstrated to be false.[11]

Bennett matched his careless remarks by attempting to ap-

[11] The American Council on Education and the National Institute of Independent Colleges and Universities examined a sample of 15,000 official stu-

point to important positions in the Department of Education two persons whose views on handicapped children were so repugnant that the secretary was himself finally constrained to withdraw their nominations. Bennett contributed to the rising apprehension about his attitudes toward education by calling on large families to do their "family planning a little better or find other means" than federal aid to send their children to college.

"TRIPLE WHAMMY"

Distressing as have been the sharp cuts in President Reagan's higher-education budgets and the damaging rhetoric of his secretary of education, alarming too were the implications for education of the "tax reform" plan the president submitted to Congress in the spring of 1985.

Provisions in the administration's original plan relating to tax-exempt bonds, charitable contributions, and the deductibility of state and local taxes would have had a devastating impact on education. The original Reagan proposals, if enacted, would have undercut the ability of colleges and universities to construct and modernize facilities, weakened incentives for private giving, and eroded the revenue base for public schools in every school district in the country.[12]

Through its efforts both to slash needed funds and to amend the tax laws, the Reagan administration would in effect subject American education to a "triple whammy." At one and the same time Mr. Reagan would, first, reduce federal monies for education programs; second, undermine the capacity of state and local governments to compensate for the shortfall;

dent records and found only one student whose family earned more than $100,000—and that a family of six children, two in college, and in heavy medical debt.

[12] A major tax reform bill did pass Congress and was signed into law on October 22, 1986. The final version of the legislation, though differing in significant ways from the original Reagan plan, contains several features damaging to higher education.

and, third, cripple efforts by schools, colleges, and universities to raise funds from private nongovernment sources.

IRONIES ABOUND

In my view, both Ronald Reagan's budget and his tax proposals stand in sharp contradiction to his own philosophy:

A president urging reductions in federal funds for education and assuming that private philanthropy and state and local governments can make up the difference wants tax changes that would reduce contributions from nonfederal sources, not increase them.

A president rhetorically committed to educational "excellence" calls for budget cuts and tax laws that would kill the drive to achieve it—an agenda for mediocrity, not quality.

A president who talks of a "society of opportunity" would deny to millions of young Americans from hard-working middle- and low-income families the opportunity to go to college.

A president who has assigned high priority to economic prosperity and a strong national defense ignores the close connection between these goals and the health of our schools, colleges, and universities.

Certainly Mr. Reagan deserves credit for lifting the level of public awareness about education, but he has not moved beyond public relations. He stresses stricter classroom discipline, more homework, better teaching, an end to drug abuse—goals with which few persons would disagree. But by holding out the tantalizing bait of such nostrums, the president is turning aside the genuine agenda for educational reform. He is diverting attention from the substantive, concrete, difficult issues of how to improve our schools and colleges. Vague statements about the "values" of education will not effectuate them. Without resources to realize values, we have but sound and fury, signifying nothing.

I am not alone in this assessment. Gerald Holton, of Harvard, one of the most active members of the Commission on Excellence whose work Mr. Reagan so often hails, writing in the fall, 1984, issue of *Daedalus,* draws particular attention to one passage of *The Nation at Risk:*

> The Federal Government [says the report] has the *primary responsibility* [italics in original] to identify the national interest in education. It should also help fund and support efforts to protect and promote that interest. It must provide the national leadership to ensure that the Nation's public and private resources are marshaled to address the issues discussed in this report.

"In my opinion," concludes Holton, "the eventual fate of educational reform in this country depends as much on the will to implement this paragraph as on any other act."

Fortunately there are heartening signs that such will exists. I have been pleased to see in the last several years a renaissance on Capitol Hill of the bipartisan coalition in support of education that characterized all of my time in Congress. The House and Senate have repeatedly rejected President Reagan's proposals to slash student aid and other education programs.

Let me make clear then that the politics of educational reform does not center on partisan differences. Rather, the battle is between, on the one hand, the bipartisan tradition of presidents and legislators of both parties who have worked together to open the doors of educational opportunity and excellence and, on the other, a narrow ideological view determined to close those doors.

Evidence for this assertion comes from Terrel Bell, secretary of education in President Reagan's first term. In a March, 1986, article in *Phi Delta Kappan,* Bell wrote of his battles while in office with "the lunatic fringes of ideological political thought" and "zealots" pressing "radical and off-the-wall ideas."

President Reagan and Secretary Bennett must be reminded

that when they attack education they are really threatening our individual freedoms, our prospects for a stronger and more competitive economy, and the security of the United States in a dangerous world.

As my colleagues, both Republicans and Democrats, on the National Commission on Student Financial Assistance and I unanimously concluded, only by bringing to its full potential the greatest of our national resources—an *educated citizenry*—can we "face and master change, . . . chart and define the future, and . . . enjoy the rich blessings of democracy secure in the knowledge that others will not create the future for us."[13]

[13]National Commission on Student Financial Assistance, *Signs of Trouble and Erosion: A Report on Graduate Education in America* (New York, 1983), p. 11.

PART THREE

EDUCATION FOR DEMOCRACY

CHAPTER 7

CHALLENGES TO LEARNING: INTERNATIONAL EDUCATION AND NATIONAL SECURITY POLICY

EDUCATION HAS BEEN A LEITMOTIV of my life. My family encouraged me, in Lyndon Johnson's phrase, to "get as much education as I could take." As a school and university student I saw how education opened doors of learning and opportunity, and much of my energy years later, as a member of Congress, was directed to keeping these doors open for others.

As a university president I have argued that it is through formal study that students enhance their lives as individuals—not only in gaining the knowledge and skills essential to a career but in developing as creative and honorable human beings. The time students spend on campus, I remind them, should help give meaning and direction to their lives even as it should increase their ability to earn a living.

There is a reason beyond individual gain that education is vital. The strength of our schools, colleges, and universities directly and profoundly affects the health of our economy, the security of our borders, and the quality, material and cultural, of our national life. Still another value of education is that without it we would not be able to live as citizens of a free, self-governing nation. Certainly no democracy can survive unless those who make choices choose wisely, and we rely on our institutions of learning to educate the citizenry and to prepare potential public leaders. For the American democracy to function requires citizens able and willing to select their representatives in government at every level; render judgments on issues of public policy; translate individual interests into larger questions of the common good; and at least for some persons, take the plunge into political activity.

Democracy and education support each other in richly symbiotic ways; the former fosters the tolerance and understanding without which a pluralistic society would explode; the latter frees the mind—and the heart—of the bounds of rigid ideology. These concluding chapters look to education as it affects the health and survival of the American democracy. The analysis covers the following terrain: first, international studies and research; second, some issues in the debate on how to protect and defend our country; and, finally, a consideration of how our political system works and why it is important to understand it.

THE CHALLENGE OF INTERNATIONAL EDUCATION

It must be obvious to all of us that none of the challenges of our day is more urgent—or more difficult—than building a structure of relationships among the nations of the world that will prevent war and encourage peace. Surely one of the ways—though not the only way—to achieve this objective is through the use of human reason, and this means education.

We live in an era when information, trade, and people move with unprecedented speed across national borders. We know that the globe on which we live is, in the universal scheme of things, small and that its regions are interdependent. Conflict in Central America, the Soviet invasion of Afghanistan, fighting in the Middle East, opposition to apartheid in South Africa—all these developments reach far across national borders.

It is not only to our defense and security that Americans' ignorance of other peoples and cultures represents a danger. Our ability to compete more effectively in the world marketplace is also at risk. The headlines remind us daily of the intensified rivalry in trade among nations and of the need to reestablish America's competitive position in what has become a genuinely global economy.

Consider these statistics:

1. In the early 1980s international trade accounted for over one-fifth of our gross national product, compared with 11 percent in 1970 and just 5 percent before World War II.

2. The product of one of every three American farms ends up in foreign markets.

3. About one-third of the profits of American corporations derives from international activity.

4. One of every five Americans depends for employment on international trade.

Strictly from the perspective of our economic interests, we must have people trained to work intelligently with Japanese trade councils, Arab oil ministries, Swiss banks, and Third World governments. In the words of the National Commission on Excellence:

> We live among determined, well educated and strongly motivated competitors. . . .
>
> The risk is not only that the Japanese make automobiles more efficiently than Americans and have government subsidies for development and export. It is not just that the South Koreans recently built the world's most efficient steel mill, or that American tools, once the pride of the world, are being displaced by German products. It is also that these developments signify a redistribution of trained capability throughout the globe. Knowledge, learning, information, and skilled intelligence are the new raw materials of international commerce and are today spreading throughout the world as vigorously as miracle drugs, synthetic fertilizers, and blue jeans did earlier. . . . Learning is the indispensable investment required for success.[1]

[1] National Commission on Excellence in Education, *A Nation at Risk: The Imperative for Education Reform* (Washington, D.C., 1983), pp. 6–7.

In such a world, how well are we preparing Americans to understand other nations, other cultures, other peoples? In my view, we are not doing very well.

FAILING GRADES

The people of the United States, in whose hands, for better or worse, lies much of the responsibility for building a peaceful and stable world, must do a far better job than we have been doing of learning about the peoples who populate the other parts of this planet. In 1979, a twenty-five-member Commission on Foreign Language and International Studies, chaired by James A. Perkins, former president of Cornell University, reported to President Carter on what the commission described as America's "scandalous incompetence" in foreign languages. The commission members declared themselves "profoundly alarmed" by the results of their inquiry. Here are just three of their findings:

1. Over 40 percent of twelfth-graders were unable to place Egypt correctly on a map, while over 20 percent were equally ignorant of the location of France or China.
2. Only 15 percent of American high school students studied a foreign language, down from 24 percent in 1965.
3. Federal officials responsible for the conduct of foreign relations expressed deep concern over decreasing foreign-language enrollments in our schools and colleges. These officials feared a lowering in the quality of new recruits and a resulting increase in the cost of providing necessary language training.

The National Commission on Excellence in Education reported that in 1980 only eight states required high schools to offer foreign-language courses and that no state insisted that students take them. The commission recommended at least two years of a foreign language in high school for college-bound students. Because language proficiency ordinarily demands four to six years of classes, the commission urged that study start in elementary school.

In another recent reminder of the languishing condition of foreign-language studies in America, the Educational Testing Service offered its Graduate Record Examination in German for the last time in December, 1983, and restricted its tests in French and Spanish to once a year. The three tests had been scheduled five times a year.

Here I again recall the report of the Subcommittee on Graduate Education of the National Commission on Student Financial Assistance. For we discovered the following:

1. The late John William Ward, of the American Council of Learned Societies, warned that we are "about to lose a generation of graduate students in foreign languages."

2. Between 1969 and 1978 federal expenditures for university-based foreign-affairs research declined from $20.3 million annually to $8.5 million, while funds for facilities dropped from $126 million in 1965 to $32 million in 1979.

3. The National Council on Foreign Language and International Studies warned of a serious deficiency of American experts on the cultures, economies, and foreign policies of Asia, sub-Saharan Africa, the Middle East, the Soviet Union, and Eastern Europe. The council declared that "the vulnerability we invite by neglecting fundamental and applied knowledge and research about foreign areas threatens our security and our commercial, diplomatic and cultural interests. Though less visible, it is no less serious than the vulnerability we would face through neglect of our military preparedness."

4. Two former directors of the Central Intelligence Agency, William Colby and Stansfield Turner, blamed lack of expert knowledge in the United States about Vietnam and Iran for serious intelligence shortcomings in those countries; both

men said that our national ignorance of Latin America appeared "almost boundless."

Not surprisingly, our commission unanimously recommended that federal support for research, instruction, and graduate study in a wide range of languages and cultures be significantly increased, and that federal support for faculty to study in foreign countries also be expanded.

As I have said earlier, in November, 1984, William J. Bennett, as chairman of the National Endowment for the Humanities, issued a report highly critical of the state of the humanities on American campuses. This document cited a sharp decline since 1966 in college entrance and graduation requirements in foreign languages. From 1966 to 1983 the percentage of colleges and universities mandating foreign-language study for admission fell from 33 to 14 percent. During the same period the percentage insisting on language study for graduation dropped from 89 to 47 percent.

In its subsequent report on the baccalaureate degree the Association of American Colleges called our "foreign language incompetence" a "national embarrassment" and included "international and multicultural experiences" in its minimum required program of study.

Two other recent reports have focused exclusively on this problem. The first, *Critical Needs in International Education: Recommendations for Action,* was produced by the National Advisory Board on International Education Programs. As secretary of education, Terrel Bell had charged this twenty-three-member panel of educators, government and business leaders, and others to develop proposals for improving foreign-language and international studies. The group concluded, "Our nation's indifference to foreign languages and cultures is unique among the advanced industrial countries and our performance in these areas lags behind that of many developing countries."

Among the nineteen recommendations of the National Advisory Board are these:

Schools should provide every student foreign language instruction in the earliest years, including an opportunity to study a language until a useful level of measured proficiency has been achieved.

Colleges and universities should require demonstrated capability in a foreign language, not simply credit hours, for admission and graduation.

Curriculum requirements at all levels, including professional schools, should be examined with a view toward exposing university students to foreign languages and international studies.

Beyond Growth: The Next Stage in Language and Area Studies was prepared by the Association of American Universities for the U.S. Department of Defense. The research team, headed by Richard Lambert, of the University of Pennsylvania, observed that "Secretary of Defense Caspar Weinberger chose language and area studies along with mathematics and science as one of the domains of higher education he felt was in greatest jeopardy of decline and of greatest interest to the nation and the Department of Defense." The AAU study found that after World War II the period of largely undirected growth in language and area studies left "vital gaps" in both research and teaching in these fields. Existing financial-aid programs are not producing enough persons knowledgeable about other countries. Students need to be trained better and longer.

Most vulnerable, according to Lambert, are the less commonly taught languages. Moreover, language expertise is found disproportionately among humanities students. In the social sciences even students in area studies neglect foreign expertise to concentrate on their disciplines, which, says

Lambert, have become "increasingly theoretical, empirical and American."

The AAU panel urged support of select universities to create critical masses of scholars in more exotic areas. The current program of federal fellowships for foreign-language and area specialists should be expanded to cover a longer period of study. In language training the report called for new "pedagogical institutes" to undertake research and train teachers; for earmarking of funds to preserve teaching of "endangered languages;" for expansion of intensive language-training facilities; and for development of an objective way of measuring language proficiency.

THE POLICY AGENDA: ACTION NEEDED NOW

At one time it appeared that we as a nation were willing to take a step toward overcoming our ignorance about the rest of the world. I was first elected to Congress in 1958, the year in which, under the leadership of President Eisenhower and with support from both Democrats and Republicans in Congress, the National Defense Education Act (NDEA) became law. The year 1958 was, of course, the year after the Soviets launched *Sputnik I* and shocked Americans into a reevaluation of the state of education in this country. One response was NDEA, an effort to regain our international leadership not only in science and mathematics but also, through Title VI of NDEA, in foreign language and area studies.

I regret to say that there has been a consistent failure to provide adequate funds for these programs. In 1980, when Title VI was expanded to embrace new activities and placed in the legislative vehicle of the Higher Education Act, the authorization for the title was slashed by more than half. These cutbacks came at the same time that the President's Commission on Foreign Languages and International Studies was urging an immediate federal expenditure of $178 million for such programs.

Nearly two decades ago Congress passed the International

Education Act, of which I was the author, which authorized grants to colleges and universities in the United States to support study and research on foreign countries and cultures and important issues in international affairs.[2] This legislation was similarly ignored in the appropriations process. Although President Lyndon Johnson signed the bill into law, Congress never voted the funds to turn our sound intentions into effective action. Yet I believe that if this commitment to international studies had been implemented we might have been far better prepared to deal with problems we have suffered in Iran, Vietnam, Central America, and elsewhere.

But America's colleges and universities are not themselves without blame. In the 1960s many of them responded to students' demands for greater flexibility and "relevance" in their courses by eliminating foreign-language requirements. Not surprisingly, many secondary schools followed suit.

It is distressing to see how the present administration in Washington, as part of its drive to slash funds for schools, colleges, and universities, has attempted to cripple or eliminate programs crucial to international studies and research. The current (fiscal 1986) appropriation for Title VI of the Higher Education Act is $32 million. The administration's latest proposed budget (for fiscal 1987) would, by seeking no money at all, eliminate this modest effort to support foreign-language and area studies.

I do not want to sound wholly alarmist, for I see several signs of hope. In 1981, Republicans and Democrats in Congress successfully joined to prevent drastic cuts in the Fulbright academic exchanges and several companion programs. The posi-

---

[2] In 1966, Chairman Adam Clayton Powell had appointed me chairman of a Task Force on International Education. For background on this legislation and this issue generally see the material produced by our task force: *International Education: Past, Present, Problems, and Prospects—Selected Readings to Accompany H.R. 14643*, 89th Cong., 2d sess., H. Doc. 527 (October, 1966); and *Hearings Before the Task Force on International Education of the Committee on Education and Labor on H.R. 12451 and H.R. 12452*, March 30, 31, April 1, 4–7,

tive outcome of this crisis demonstrated that there continues to be a strong and vocal constituency in America for such measures.

One of the most articulate and effective legislators in this area, Senator Paul Simon (D.-Ill.), has pressed several measures in Congress to enhance foreign-language training and the study of other cultures. He has also labored, so far successfully, to prevent reductions in present Title VI programs. Senator Simon's views on the need for greater commitment to international education, especially foreign languages, in the United States are contained in his excellent book *The Tongue-tied American.*[3]

On another front, Senator Richard G. Lugar, chairman of the Senate Foreign Relations Committee, and Congressman Lee Hamilton, chairman of the House Select Committee on Intelligence and a senior member of the Foreign Affairs Committee—both from Indiana, the former a Republican, the latter a Democrat—jointly introduced legislation, the Soviet-Eastern European Research and Training Act, to address another serious concern. Between 1968 and 1982 government and private support of Soviet studies in the United States suffered, in constant dollars, a 77 percent decline. The Soviet Union today has roughly three times as many people working on United States foreign policy as we do on Soviet foreign affairs.

The Lugar-Hamilton measure, which Congress passed in December, 1983, authorizes a $50 million endowment to support, over a ten-year period, fellowships and assistant professorships in Soviet and Eastern European studies. If Congress appropriated the funds to make real the promise of the new program, the result could significantly strengthen American capabilities in a field crucial to our national security.

1966. See also the report that accompanied the International Education Act of 1966, 89th Cong., 2d sess., H. Rept. 1539 (May 17, 1966).

[3] Paul Simon, *The Tongue-tied American: Confronting the Foreign Language Crisis* (New York: Continuum, 1980).

Beyond these initiatives, there have been other heartening developments. Many colleges and universities—including Harvard, the University of Pennsylvania, Emory University, Middlebury College, and the University of Massachusetts—are reinstituting language requirements for graduation. A recent survey conducted by the Modern Language Association indicated that, in a reversal of a twelve-year trend, enrollments in foreign-language courses in American colleges and universities are now rising.

There has also been a resurgence of interest in foreign languages in elementary and secondary schools. The New York State Board of Regents, for example, now requires three years of a foreign language for a regents' diploma, a goal pursued by nearly half the state's high school graduates, and, by grade nine, two years of foreign language study for all students.

All these endeavors—at every level—enrich the international perspective of young Americans and help prepare them for work and life in a world that will never be narrow again.

NATIONAL SECURITY POLICY

Even as the United States must give more support to international studies and research, another area to which the country's leaders, educated men and women generally, and our colleges and universities in particular must pay far greater attention is national-security policy. The defense budget of the United States has become so consequential to the lives of us all, to the economy of the country, and to the nature of our society that we must now lift the subject to a far higher level of national debate—and national understanding.

Obviously issues of war and peace are vastly more complicated than ever before. To comprehend them, we must know more facts, take into account more variables, and, in developing national policy, far more skillfully balance means and goals.

The Preamble of the Constitution of the United States declares one of the basic purposes of our government to be "to provide for the common defense." That there is a widespread consensus in the United States that we must have a strong defense to ensure our freedoms in a dangerous world, few would deny. But in recent years—during administrations of both political parties—there have been more and more questions about the objectives of our defense policy and the methods by which we as a nation make decisions about our security needs.

BILLIONS FOR DEFENSE

Consider the magnitude of defense in the overall budget of the government of the United States. The years 1982 to 1985 saw the largest peacetime military buildup in history. From fiscal 1982 to 1985 we provided for defense more than $1,007,900,000,000—one trillion, seven billion, nine hundred million dollars. In fiscal 1986 alone the Pentagon will receive nearly $300 billion. Whether these amounts are too much or too little money for defense is not the question I raise here. My questions are more fundamental still:

How do we *know* how much to spend on defense?
What is the *process* by which we come to judgments on our defense expenditures?
What is the *impact* of our defense budget on the nation's life?

Clearly, the hundreds of billions of dollars expended for national security affect the country in a diversity of ways. Spending on defense has repercussions for the national economy, for scientific and industrial research, for our supply of educated manpower, for our colleges and universities. The defense budget directly affects the lives of all Americans— as employers and employees, as taxpayers, as fathers and mothers, as sons and daughters, as students and teachers.

The size and scope of the defense budget raise large, complex but crucial questions:

What is the economic impact of substantial flows of defense dollars—or the lack of such dollars—on different communities and regions of the country? On people of various income groups, ages, and occupations?

How do we integrate the foreign-policy objectives of the United States with our military strategy?

What, in the making of such judgments, are the appropriate roles of the president; of the secretaries of state, defense, and treasury; of the national security adviser and the director of the CIA?

What is the responsibility of Congress, which under Article I of the Constitution has the responsibility "to declare war, . . . to raise and support armies, . . . to provide and maintain a navy," in the making of defense policy?

During my time on Capitol Hill, I observed that only a few legislators were in any significant way involved in decisions that affected the nation's destiny in this most fundamental area, security policy.

I recall one of the first meetings my colleagues and I, as members of the leadership of the House of Representatives, had with President Carter at the White House. The president asked whether any of us wanted a briefing on any subject. I replied that I felt that the House leaders should have an opportunity to talk with the secretary of defense. A session with Secretary Harold Brown was arranged, with both Democratic and Republican House Leaders present, in the office of the Speaker of the House, Thomas P. O'Neill, Jr. (D.-Mass.).

The Speaker opened the discussion by telling Dr. Brown, "I have been a member of the House Leadership for six years, and this is the first time I have been briefed by a Secretary of Defense." The Speaker of the House of Representatives is the second most powerful official of the government of the United States. During my own years of service only members of the Armed Services Committee and Defense Appropriations

Subcommittee had significant access to the information and intelligence necessary to reach sound judgments on the making of defense policy. This small circle widens, of course, if we add the senior military and national-security officials in the executive branch. Yet the overall numbers of those with knowledge of and substantial influence on the decisions that affect the security of the country remain a tiny fraction of the policymakers.

Because in a free and democratic society judgments involving national-security policy require thoughtful and well-informed scrutiny by citizens, every educated person has a particular obligation to think seriously about so vital a matter as our national defense. Indeed, in the past few years questions of foreign and defense policy have moved to the forefront of national debate:

Beginning with the nuclear freeze movement in 1983, continuing through the Reagan administration's Strategic Defense Initiative to the Reykjavík talks between President Reagan and Soviet leader Mikhail Gorbachev in October, 1986, national attention has been increasingly drawn to issues of arms control and relations between the United States and the Soviet Union.

Deepening United States involvement in Central America has sparked periodic confrontation between President Reagan and Congress.

Evidence of staggering cost overruns and procurement mismanagement by the Pentagon has caused mounting criticism from Congress and the public.

Dramatic debates and close votes in Congress have accompanied decisions on an array of weapons: the MX missile, the B-1 bomber, and binary nerve gas.

I must insist here that I am neither attacking nor endorsing the defense expenditures now being projected. Nor am I opposing or advocating the weapons systems that I have mentioned. My point is different, namely, that the size and scope of our defense budget; the complexities of modern weapons, both conventional and nuclear, as well as of arms-control issues; the risks and dangers we face in foreign affairs—all these factors challenge us to confront these questions: How does the government of the United States determine security policy? How competently does the government make these decisions?

Fortunately these questions have begun to attract the attention of some knowledgeable and respected legislators, as well as a presidential commission. For example, in a remarkable set of speeches delivered in Congress in the fall of 1985, Senators Barry Goldwater (R.-Ariz.) and Sam Nunn (D.-Ga.) undertook a comprehensive survey of the nation's defense capabilities and said what they thought was wrong with the defense establishment. As then chairman and ranking minority member, respectively, of the Armed Services Committee, these two leaders were powerful voices for reform. Their criticisms touched on interservice rivalries, lack of strategic planning, and corruption in weapons buying. The two senators translated their ideas into a single Pentagon reorganization bill, which Congress passed and is now law. A key feature of the legislation seeks to lessen interservice conflict by strengthening the chairman of the Joint Chiefs of Staff.

In the House of Representatives, Congressman Les Aspin (D.-Wis.), chairman of the Armed Services Committee, has also drawn attention to inefficiencies in Pentagon practices, recently holding hearings to assess what the nation has received for its expenditure since 1981 of $1 trillion on defense.

In June, 1985, President Reagan appointed a Blue Ribbon Commission on Defense Management, chaired by David K. Packard, a former deputy secretary of defense who now heads Hewlett-Packard, to examine the current structure and operation of the Pentagon and recommend changes. The bipartisan Packard group finished its work in 1986 with several stinging criticisms of the nation's military establishment. The commission declared, for example, "There is no rational system whereby the executive branch and the Congress reach coherent and enduring agreement on national military strategy, the forces to carry it out, and the funding that should be provided." Again, "There is no uniformed officer clearly responsible" for providing an integrated picture of "the nation's combatant commanders."

In addition, the commission asserted:

> There is legitimate cause for dissatisfaction with the process by which the Department of Defense and Congress buy military equipment and material. . . . numerous reports of questionable procurement practices have fostered a conviction, widely shared by members of the public and by many in government, that defense contractors place profits above legal and ethical responsibilities.[4]

Several of the proposals made by the Packard commission for better coordination of the activities of the various military services and for streamlining the Pentagon procurement system were similar to the Goldwater-Nunn initiatives and were already contained in their legislation.

Clearly, considerable ferment is brewing in both branches of government and in both political parties about how to make the soundest decisions for the nation's security. But equally clearly, in my view, this debate should not be confined to government circles.

A ROLE FOR UNIVERSITIES

Nor is it enough simply to exhort citizens, no matter how well educated or informed, to pay more attention to the framing of defense policy. People need help. Leaders in government, business, and industry and others responsible for making de-

---

[4] President's Blue Ribbon Commission on Defense Management (Washington, D.C., July, 1986).

cisions about our national security require an analytical framework within which they can intelligently think about policy.

Here is a special obligation for colleges and universities.
One of the reasons for the existence of a university, after all, is
to encourage systematic, objective, and disciplined reflection
about complex problems. It is, in my judgment, time to bring
the capabilities of our institutions of higher learning to bear
on the entire spectrum of issues involved in the making of
policy for our national defense.

I reiterate that I am not here concerned about whether there
should be a B-1 bomber or an MX missile, or a SALT or a
START arms-control strategy. I am pressing neither a hawkish
nor a dovish position. Rather I am urging our colleges and
universities to find ways to stimulate a broader, deeper, more
thorough understanding of the structure of decision making
for the security policies of the United States.

Universities could, for example, offer lectures, seminars,
conferences, and courses on the subject. Among the partici-
pants should be persons who have served in key positions in
the White House and the Departments of Defense and State
and the intelligence agencies, as well as members of the
House and Senate knowledgeable about defense matters.
Leaders in business and industry, finance, and labor should
participate, and so, too, of course, should university professors from the disciplines of economics and political science, physics and mathematics, sociology and psychology,
history and anthropology, and, I believe, philosophy and the-
ology. Such activities should be carried out at a number of
universities across the country. The value of such engagement
in the national-security debate by university-based scholars
is twofold. First, their participation would widen the context
within which military and strategic topics are considered. For,
historically, issues of war and peace have been inextricably
linked to a wide diversity of forces—changing forms of government, shifting economic and demographic trends, the

rise and decline of belief systems and styles of behavior. Certainly in the nuclear age, when the security decisions of one nation, ours or another, can have global implications, it is absurd—and dangerous—for policymakers to make judgments about defense in less than the broadest, richest, intellectual environment.

The second reason to encourage leading thinkers from all fields to turn their attention to defense and security questions has to do with the methods and standards of the academy. The fundamental privilege of university life is freedom—freedom to conduct research, to explore avenues of inquiry wherever they may lead, to be open to alternative explanations—and all in the spirit of the unfettered pursuit of knowledge. This privilege in turn engenders obligations, the most basic of which is adherence to the norms of rigorous scholarship and intellectual integrity. In my view the involvement of our universities in the consideration of the shaping of defense and security policies generally would bring more openness, greater illumination, and deeper insight to a dimension of American life that, though of fundamental importance to our people and all humankind, remains little understood.

CHAPTER 8

UNDERSTANDING AMERICAN POLITICS: THE IMPERATIVES OF CITIZENSHIP

DEMOCRACY, AS A FORM OF GOVERNMENT, places a premium on an informed citizenry. In a democratic society there is no king, absolute ruler, or single authority who does all the thinking and makes all the choices. The people themselves, acting chiefly through their elected representatives, make the basic decisions about how they will be governed. In such a system education, which Thomas Jefferson defined as that which "enables every man to judge for himself what secures or endangers freedom," is crucial.

Yet for Americans to exercise reasoned judgments about their government they must have at least a modicum of understanding of our political arrangements. This is no easy task. Even knowledgeable, sophisticated citizens often display remarkable ignorance of the processes by which the nation is governed.

I have attempted in earlier chapters to suggest the complexity and richness of one part of our system of government, Congress. The theme of this chapter, accordingly, is that we must devote much more attention to teaching, especially at the college and university level, about our political institutions and the ways in which we govern ourselves.

THE AMERICAN "MAZE"

Basic to an appreciation of the American form of government is a recognition of certain fundamental factors. First, our Constitution is characterized by the separation of powers. Second, our political parties are decentralized. To these two traditional ingredients must be added a third—a change in the nature of Congress itself, especially in the House of Representatives.

People know the phrase "separation of powers" from their civics lessons, but too few understand its meaning. Some seem to think that in the American system Congress exists to do whatever a president wants it to. In this view a president asks, and Congress gives. But this is not the way the Founding Fathers intended the government of the United States to work, and in recent years Congress has reaffirmed the principle of separation of powers by reasserting its constitutional role in the making of both domestic and foreign policy.

There is another complicating factor: presidents and Congresses are elected separately. The president, each senator, and each member of the House of Representatives has his or her own mandate and sense of responsibility to the people. Some members of Congress like to recall Speaker Rayburn's reply when asked how many presidents he had served under. Retorted Mr. Rayburn, "None! But I have had the privilege of serving *with* eight presidents." I served *with* six—three Democrats, three Republicans.

In our system, as distinguished from a parliamentary democracy, the chief executive is not chosen from among the legislative majority and, indeed, often does not even belong to the majority party in Congress. This is, of course, precisely the situation in the United States today with a Republican in the White House and Democrats in control of both the Senate and the House of Representatives.

The White House and Congress are thus occupied by persons often elected for different reasons and by constituencies with varying expectations and demands. The American way of governing was not designed for peaceful coexistence between the executive and legislative branches. Nor have political realities done much to eliminate the potential for tension between them.

The result of this constitutional arrangement has been a process, nearly two centuries long, of conflict and accommodation, dispute and detente. In fact, one branch of the government invades the sphere of the other so often that we have not a complete separation of powers but rather, as Harvard's Richard Neustadt has put it, "separated institutions sharing powers." Separation of powers, then, is one characteristic that sets the American political system apart from that of most other democratic nations.

DECLINE OF PARTIES

The second factor is equally important, for to speak of an active role for "Congress" assumes a Congress acting with a single mind. This is often far from the case, chiefly because we do not have highly disciplined political parties. Our decentralized party system affects, in important ways, the relationships between presidents and congresses. Our two traditional major political parties in the United States have made possible durable coalitions of disparate but broadly compatible interests. Groups with substantially different goals have found common advantage under the broad umbrella of party. Moreover, perhaps because of their internal diversity, American political parties have historically served as instruments for developing consensus across the spectrum of major issues. In a country so large and with such a variety of differences of region, religion, race, ethnic origin, and economic interest, this role is essential.

We have, however, been witnessing a significant decline in loyalties to even these relatively undisciplined parties. This drop in party allegiance is evident both in the population as a whole and among members of Congress. Each year fewer and fewer Americans classify themselves, when asked, as "Democrats" or "Republicans." Instead they call themselves "Independents"—a trend, by the way, I do *not* applaud.

In Congress itself, although the level of party affiliation remains high, the degree of party discipline often does not. As a former Majority Whip, I speak on this point with authority and not as the scribes. If I were chief government whip in the British House of Commons, my major responsibility would be to ensure that on important votes the members of Parliament of my party were physically present. Save in exceptional cases, I would know with certainty how the MPs would vote. But in the U.S. House of Representatives the majority party has an elaborate organization of more than fifty whips—all Democratic members—simply to find out *how* their Democratic colleagues intend to vote—and, should they prove indecisive, recalcitrant, hostile, or in some instances negotiable, seek to persuade them to support the party leadership.

For example, in the first year of the Reagan presidency, in votes in the House of Representatives on the administration's key budget and tax proposals, almost 20 percent (one-fifth) of the Democratic members abandoned their party leadership's position to vote with the Republicans. After the 1982 elections, however, with twenty-six more Democrats in the House, Mr. Reagan was not able to sustain his winning streak, largely because of defections from *his* own party. This pattern held after the 1984 elections. The president had particular difficulty in retaining the support of his fellow Republicans in the Senate, twenty-two of whom faced reelection in 1986. For these senators the pull of loyalty to a president of their party was offset by the demands of their own electoral politics.

There are several reasons for the weakening of party ties in the United States. Even while expanding the impact of the presidency, television has enabled members of Congress to bypass traditional local party organizations and go directly to the people for support. Moreover, the sheer complexity of the American nation contributes to the challenge of holding members of Congress of the same party together on issues, both foreign and domestic. The United States is so large, populous, and diverse that on many questions—for example, energy, environment, or trade policy—regional or economic factors rather than partisan considerations predominate.

As the institution of party recedes from its primacy in our political system, party organizations are more and more being supplanted by special-interest and political-action committees (PACs). Many of these entities concentrate on a single issue to the exclusion of all others, assigning their support to a candidate or withholding it solely on the basis of his or her position on that particular issue—abortion, for example, or gun control or school busing. So expensive has become the cost of modern campaigning that candidates for Congress increasingly rely on contributions from the special-interest PACs—yet another force that diminishes the power of party.

Beyond the reassertion of a congressional role in a separation-of-powers system and the decline of already decentralized parties, there is a third factor that has altered the functioning of contemporary American politics: the new composition and new style of the post-Vietnam, post-Watergate Congress.

THE NEW CONGRESS

This development is, of course, closely linked to renewed congressional assertiveness. The members of today's House and Senate are significantly different from those who served there when I first went to Congress over twenty-five years ago. The newer members—and I speak more knowledgeably of the House members—are young, intelligent, well educated, hardworking, and skeptical. In the House of Representatives today some 164 members—almost 40 percent—have served two terms or less. Fully three-fourths of the members of the House and two-thirds of the members of the Senate have been elected since Richard Nixon resigned the presidency in August, 1974. These new men and women bring both new vigor and new difficulties. With this House it is not possible for either presidents or Speakers easily to have their way. Neither the White House nor House leaders can prevail by edict or command. To convince members today, it is necessary to rely on reason and persuasion.

There has also been a profound change in the legendary committee structure of the House. The chairmanships of thirty to forty subcommittees, where the bulk of the legislative work is done, are in the hands of relatively junior members. Because ascension to committee leadership is no longer assured by seniority, committee chairmen, once nearly all-powerful, must now pay heed both to the members of their committees and to their party colleagues in the House. To be effective today, a committee chairman must operate like a politician, not an autocrat.

These are among the changes in the operation of the House that have made it more open, more democratic, more accountable—and I strongly supported them when I was a member of Congress. These reforms have also, however, extracted a price in terms of the time and effort required to get things done, no trivial consideration in a period when the sheer volume of problems that must be addressed by government threatens to grow beyond manageability. The decline of party and the more diffuse power structure of the House make all the more complicated the task not only of the president but of the leadership of the House in putting together majorities for both domestic and foreign-policy legislation.

The American system of governing—and I have focused on the institution I know best, the House of Representatives—is not easy to fathom, even, I must observe, for some presidents of the United States.

EDUCATION FOR DEMOCRACY

Beyond the intrinsic satisfaction of understanding a complex system, so crucial to the future of our country is a vigorous and viable national goverment that it is imperative that thoughtful citizens understand its workings. We need more first-class scholars of the American way of governing and particularly of "our first branch of government," Congress. Not only must we support scholarship at our universities, but we must encourage citizens to inform themselves on matters political. The kind of knowledge required, however, comes not only from formal study but also from *doing*—from active engagement in the arena of politics. For most Americans who aspire to what we may call "civic competence," this engagement will involve action in one of our two major parties—and to this I say, "Bravo!"

Alexis de Tocqueville over a century and a half ago drew a stunning portrait of how the civically competent American responded on being questioned about his country. Wrote the visiting Frenchman:

> [The American's] language will become as clear and precise as his thoughts. He will inform you what his rights are and by what means he exercises them; he will be able to point out the customs which obtain in the political world. You will find that he is well acquainted with the rules of the administration, and that he is familiar with the mechanism of the laws. The citizen of the United States does not acquire his practical science and his positive notions from books. . . . The American learns to know the laws by participating in the act of legislation; and he takes a lesson in the form of government from governing. The great work of society is ever going on before his eyes and as it were, under his hands.[1]

Our form of government derives its legitimacy and its strength from a citizen body that is both knowledgeable and willing to act on that knowledge. When the latest figures show that only half the Americans eligible to vote do so, we may reasonably ask how far our democracy has moved away from the one de Tocqueville described.

I shall go a step further to voice the hope that more well-educated, highly motivated young Americans will, as they con-

[1] Alexis de Tocqueville, *Democracy in America*, 1st Borzoi ed. (New York: Alfred A. Knopf, 1945), 1:318.

sider their careers, decide to take the plunge into the rough and tumble of electoral politics and, more specifically still, that they will run for Congress. I know that some tremble at the thought of the controversy and criticism that the assumption of political office may entail. But allow me to say, from the perspective of one who has done so, that there is satisfaction in being involved, even with but one voice and vote, in decisions that shape the future of our country and the world. There is attraction, in this age of specialization, in a life that touches, even if tangentially, on a wide range of subjects, from minimum wage to Medicare, from farm policy to foreign policy. And there is excitement in the exercise of one's abilities along lines that afford scope for individual achievement of worthy goals.

The attractions and rewards of a life of public service were aptly captured more than a dozen years ago by the person whose words I invoked at the beginning of this book. On January 3, 1973, Congressman Carl Albert of Oklahoma addressed the members of the House of Representatives, who had just elected him to a second term as Speaker. Mr. Albert's words then say eloquently what I have tried to communicate through these pages:

> My colleagues, I see America as a nation constantly in motion, striving, growing, building, dreaming, playing, changing, planning, reforming. I see an America that is not an end in itself, but a great and noble experiment for the betterment of all mankind.
>
> I see Congress as a part of that experiment, not the roadblock to change, but an instrument of orderly and thoughtful progress. I see each of us, 435 elected Members of this body, carrying on our tasks and adding to the treasured sweep of American history.

INDEX